The Power of the
Bulleid
Light Pacifics

Undoubtedly one of the most impressive trains to run on British Railways after Nationalisation was the 'Golden Arrow', particularly when equipped with all the embellishments. An immaculate No 34103 *Calstock* makes a superb sight as it passes Knockholt in 1951 with the down train. *F. R. Hebron / Rail Archive Stephenson*

The Power of the

Bulleid
Light Pacifics

Gavin Morrison

An imprint of
Ian Allan Publishing

Contents

Frontispiece: Only four months before being withdrawn, No 34051 *Winston Churchill* prepares to leave Leamington Spa on 23 May 1965 with a Stephenson Locomotive Society special from Birmingham Snow Hill. No 34051 worked the special as far as Salisbury, which was its home shed at the time. The locomotive is now preserved in the National Collection. *Gavin Morrison*

Title page: No 21C101 pictured when new. It received the name *Exeter* at an official ceremony held at the city's Central station on 10 July 1945. It entered traffic on 21 June 1945. *Ian Allan Library*

First published 2008

ISBN (10) 0 86093 621 X
ISBN (13) 978 0 86093 621 3

Published by Oxford Publishing Co

an imprint of Ian Allan Publishing Ltd, Hersham, Surrey, KT12 4RG
Printed in England by Ian Allan Printing Ltd, Hersham, Surrey, KT12 4RG

Code: 0807/B

Visit the Ian Allan Publishing website at www.ianallanpublishing.com

Introduction

Having recently published *The Power of the Merchant Navies* on the basis of showing each locomotive in rebuilt and unrebuilt form, I thought it would be a challenge to see if I could do the same for the 'West Country' and 'Battle of Britain' class. Obtaining examples of the 30 'Merchant Navy' class locomotives was easy but, as I was to find out, 110 unrebuilt and 60 rebuilt locomotives turned out to be far more difficult than I had envisaged. Having done a number of books in the 'Power' series, it is uncanny how certain locos are so camera shy. In the case of this book unrebuilt 'West Country' No 34026 was by far the most difficult; I have, however, achieved it, although with an extra 16 pages being necessary, for which I thank the publishers.

In spite of the very troublesome period with the introduction of the 'Merchant Navy' class O. V. S. Bulleid pressed ahead with the introduction of the lightweight Pacifics, a type that incorporated all the features (good or bad) of the 'Merchant Navy' class but on a slightly smaller scale. The big difference this time round, however, was that the crews, shed staff and works had all gone through a very sharp learning curve with the 'Merchant Navies' so were well prepared for the Light Pacifics.

The type's initial use was to be in the West Country, an area which had been struggling on for years with 'T9s' and 'Ns', and the new locomotives were designed for mixed traffic duties. The Pacifics were far more powerful than was needed west of Exeter, but it was realised that, after the war, electrification was going to be many years away in the southeast and more powerful locomotives were certainly going to be needed in this area. To Bulleid's credit he took the decision that it would be better to have one class to cover all the needs of the Southern except minor branch lines, rather than two or three different classes, even if the locomotives were bigger or more powerful than necessary for many of the duties.

Apart from six members of the class, all the locomotives were built in Brighton (the others at Eastleigh). All the 'Merchant Navy' features were present: the oil bath to enclose the motion, thermic siphons, BFB wheel centres, patent valve gear and the familiar air smooth casing. All of these features had been designed to ease and reduce maintenance.

In a well-managed public relations exercise, the Southern Railway presented No 21C101 at Exeter Central to the public on 9 July 1945 where it was named *Exeter*. Painted in malachite-green livery, the locomotive really captured the public's imagination after all the war years of drab black livery. No 21C101's trials went reasonably smoothly apart from a boiler problem that was quickly sorted. The engines entered service with tenders with capacity for 4,500 gallons of water and five tons of coal. Compared to the 'Merchant

Navies' locomotive weight was reduced from 94¾ tons to 86 tons, due partly to the considerable amount of welding employed in construction.

The cab width was reduced from 9ft on the 'Merchant Navies' to 8ft 6in for Nos 21C101-63; locomotives in this range that were rebuilt had this increased to 9ft. The class was designed to be used on the Tonbridge–Hastings route with its restricted clearance, although this never actually happened. A problem, as on the 'Merchant Navies', was that of drifting smoke, which together with the smoke-deflectors and small front cab window, made visibility difficult for the crews. Several trials were carried out, but none really solved the problem with the unrebuilt locomotives, although the fitting of a 'wedge'-shape frontal cab with larger windows was of some assistance.

Another masterstroke by the Public Relations department was the decision to name the locomotives from No 21C149 onwards, after Battle of Britain squadrons, fighter planes and famous people associated with World War 2. To some people this created another class but in truth the locomotives were identical, although the publicity surrounding all the events at the naming ceremonies around the Southern helped maintain the public's interest.

The locomotives selected to take part in the 1948 Locomotive Exchanges took the type to areas of the country where it had never been before, such as the Highland and the London Midland lines. The performance of the locomotives completely outclassed the competition, supposed to be of equivalent size and power, but, it has to be admitted, at the expense of vast quantities of coal being consumed.

Shortly after Nationalisation it was realised that the Southern Region was awash with Light Pacifics, and trials were organised with locomotive No 34059 on the Great Eastern section of the Eastern Region with a view to the possible transfer of some of the class to work the expresses out of Liverpool Street. The management on the Great Eastern was fully aware of the impending arrival of the 'Britannias' and had made up their mind that this is what they intended to have, so, whilst the trials with No 34059 certainly proved that it was vastly superior to anything already on the Great Eastern, politics played their part, and the Great Eastern got its 'Britannias', its case no doubt helped by the fact that No 34059 caught fire whilst on loan.

Initially the locomotives entered service in the striking malachite-green livery. After Nationalisation a number were repainted apple green prior to the adoption of BR green as standard. All of the locomotives were ultimately to receive this livery, although it was not until the early 1950s that malachite green was finally eliminated.

The tenders moved around between locomotives, there were several modifications resulting from rebuilding as a result of corrosion. The main difference was the removal on all but five of the raves, which

Below: After 12 years' service No 34001 *Exeter* was rebuilt in November 1957. Here it is seen approaching Poole station as it heads an up Channel Island train from Weymouth to Waterloo on 29 July 1966. *Gavin Morrison*

hindered the crews when taking water and were always getting damaged.

In hindsight it is clear that the Light Pacifics, like the 'Merchant Navies', had very advanced features, some of which never really produced the benefits they were designed to achieve. There is no doubt that, in both forms, they were complete masters of the jobs they were allocated to perform and, from my observations from the late 1950s, they seemed to perform easily the duties allocated to the 'Merchant Navies'. Why so many were built, when the BR Standards were just about to appear, and why Stewarts Lane shed was allocated two 'Britannias' for 'Golden Arrow' duties when there were plenty of Light Pacifics around seem mysteries to me.

As with the 'Merchant Navies', it was eventually decided to solve all the problems associated with the Bulleid design and rebuild 60 members of the class. This certainly improved availability as well as reliability and running costs, but did not really produce a locomotive with a better performance than the unrebuilt version when it was working well.

Some of the rebuilds had very short careers and the cost involved in rebuilding was hardly justified. However, to be fair it was envisaged that steam would last longer than it did on the region.

The entire class of 110 locomotives was withdrawn over a period of four years between 1963 and 1967, but fortunately two were preserved straight from service, while others finished up at Dai Woodham's scrapyard at Barry, from which they would subsequently be rescued. As a result the preservation movement has finished up with arguably more examples than necessary, the survivors numbering some 20 locomotives — 10 unrebuilt and 10 rebuilt.

I have deliberately not included a section on the preserved examples as we see them in action every month in the magazines, out on the main line and the private railways.

As always I will conclude by thanking the photographers who have gone to considerable trouble to produce a picture of every locomotive in both rebuilt and unrebuilt forms, and I hope that you enjoy this photographic album.

Gavin Morrison
Mirfield
January 2008

Bibliography
The Book of the West Country and Battle of Britain Pacifics by Richard Derry (Irwell Press, 2002)
Bulleid Locomotives by Brian Haresnape (Ian Allan, 1977)
Locomotives of the Southern Railway, Part 2 (Railway Correspondence & Travel Society, 1976)

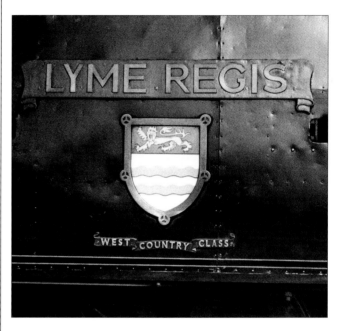

Above: Nameplate, crest and scroll as fited to No 34009 *Lyme Regis. Brian Morrison*

Below: Rebuilt and unrebuilt examples pictured side-by-side at Semley on 8 June 1964. On the left No 34107 *Blandford Forum* leaves with an Exeter–Salisbury local, whilst on the right No 34032 *Camelford* waits with a brake van in the goods yard. *Derek Cross*

Left: No 34005 *Barnstaple*, the first of the class to be rebuilt (in June 1957), is recorded at Southampton Central with an up express on 12 September 1966. *Gavin Morrison*

Below: No 34002 *Salisbury* pictured in the yard just outside Chichester station after working a special from London and waiting to take it forward to Portsmouth, after it had travelled over the Lavant branch, on 3 October 1965. *Gavin Morrison*

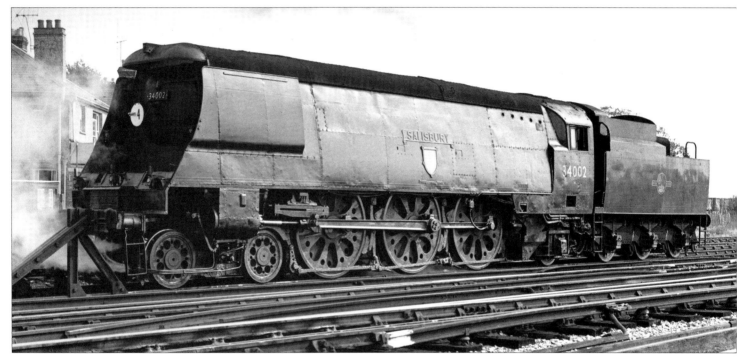

Right: Looking well cleaned but without its *Yeovil* nameplate, No 34004 awaits its next duty at Weymouth shed on 7 May 1967, two months before withdrawal. *Gavin Morrison*

Left: The entire class was built at
Brighton between 1945 and 1951,
except for Nos 34095/7/9/101/2/4,
which were built at Eastleigh.
In early 1945 No 21C103 has just
had the boiler, which was to operate
at 280lb/sq in, with the evaporative
and superheating surfaces at 2,122sq
ft and 545sq ft respectively,
mounted on the frames inside
Brighton Works.
Pendragon Collection

Below: A view inside Eastleigh
Works in early 1945 shows
No 21C102 virtually complete and
another 'West Country' taking
shape.
Ian Allan Library

Under Construction

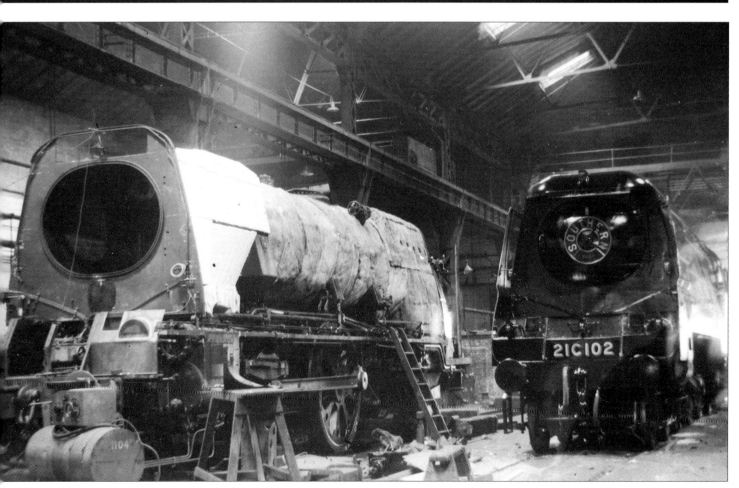

Right: A partially completed 'West Country' is seen alongside No 21C102, later to be named *Salisbury*, in early 1945. *Ian Allan Library*

Left: Another view inside Brighton Works, on 12 July 1945, featuring No 21C105 (later named *Barnstaple* and subsequently the first of the class to be rebuilt) in the final stages of construction. *W. Beckerlegge / Rail Archive Stephenson*

Below: The finished product outside Brighton Works pictured around the end of August 1947, resplendent in the impressive malachite-green livery. No 21C167 *Tangmere*, which was not rebuilt, can today be seen running on the main line on specials. *Rail Archive Stephenson*

The Locomotives

21C101 *Exeter*

Entered service:	21 June 1945
Renumbered:	34001, March 1949
BR green livery:	December 1949
'Wedge' cab fitted:	January 1953
Mileage (unrebuilt):	584,794
Rebuilt:	November 1957
Mileage (rebuilt):	495,163
Mileage (total):	1,079,957
Withdrawn:	July 1967
Fate:	Cut up Cashmores, Newport, October 1967

Below: Exeter went new to Exmouth Junction shed and remained allocated there until 8 October 1957. It is shown here leaving Templecombe on 6 June 1949 with a down slow passenger train for Exeter, having received a front numberplate but retaining the malachite-green livery, albeit without any tender lettering. *J. P. Watson / Rail Archive Stephenson*

Left: Without a trace of exhaust on a hot summer's day, No 34001 heads an up cross-country express near Hinton Admiral in the New Forest on 23 July 1966. Although it was to last for another year, No 34001 is in poor external condition and has lost its nameplates. Signs of the pending Bournemouth electrification can be seen on the trackbed.
Gavin Morrison

21C102 *Salisbury*

Entered service:	June 1945
Renumbered:	34002, November 1948
BR green livery:	October 1949
'Wedge' cab fitted:	June 1951
Mileage (total):	1,003,613
Withdrawn:	April 1967
Fate:	Cut up Cashmores, Newport, October 1967

Right: The external condition of *Salisbury* is hardly appropriate for the down 'Bournemouth Belle' Pullman, which it is hauling past Dunsford Road on 8 November 1964. Allocated to Eastleigh at the time, it is possible that No 34002 was covering for a failed Nine Elms locomotive, which normally provided the power for the train. *Salisbury* achieved the longest time in service for an unrebuilt member of the class — 21 years 10 months. *Brian Stephenson*

21C103 *Plymouth*

Entered service:	June 1945
Renumbered:	34003, May 1948
BR green livery:	March 1952
'Wedge' cab fitted:	September 1953
Mileage (unrebuilt):	543,328
Rebuilt:	September 1957
Mileage (rebuilt):	268,346
Mileage (total):	811,674
Withdrawn:	September 1964
Fate:	Cut up at Woods, Queenborough, December 1964

Above: This picture taken in the early 1950s shows *Plymouth* crossing the River Taw estuary at Barnstaple heading for Junction station with an Ilfracombe-Exeter Central local train. *Neville Stead collection*

Left: Some 1½ miles south west of Milborne Port, near Sherborne, on 18 May 1964, No 34003 is at the head of an up express. *M. Mensing*

Left: No 34001 was chosen as the locomotive to represent the class in the Locomotive Exchanges of 1948 in Scotland. It had recently had a general repair and was fitted with a wedge-shaped cab and longer smoke-deflectors. It was attached to an LMS 4,000gal tender and underwent further modifications before operation in Scotland, including the fitting of a tablet-catcher for working the Highland line. It worked the 4pm Perth–Inverness and 8.20am Inverness–Perth. Its performance was superb, but at the expense of coal consumption. It is shown here backing the coaches from Glasgow Buchanan Street onto the rest of the train at Perth before heading north during the trials in July 1948. *Pendragon Collection*

21C104 *Yeovil*

Entered service:	30 June 1945
'Wedge' cab fitted:	March 1948
Renumbered:	34004, May 1948
BR green livery:	April 1950
Mileage (unrebuilt):	573,593
Rebuilt:	February 1958
Mileage (rebuilt):	347,379
Mileage (total):	920,972
Withdrawn:	July 1967
Fate:	Cut up Cashmores, Newport, October 1962

Below: Passing Milepost 109¾ from Waterloo, a very dirty Eastleigh-allocated No 34004 heads an up express between Bournemouth Central and Gas Works Junction on 1 September 1965. *Gavin Morrison*

21C105 *Barnstaple*

Entered service:	July 1945
'Wedge' cab fitted:	May 1948
Renumbered:	34005, May 1948
BR green livery:	May 1950
Mileage (unrebuilt):	489,808
Rebuilt:	June 1957
Mileage (rebuilt):	347,524
Mileage (total):	837,332
Withdrawn:	October 1966
Fate:	Cut up Buttigiegs, Newport, October 1967

Left: Barnstaple, recorded *c*1947 with Southern on the tender and numbered 21C105. It is fitted with an indicator shelter for test purposes whilst allocated to Exmouth Junction. *H. M. Madgwick*

Right: Now numbered 34005, it is shown nine months prior to rebuilding at its then home shed at Nine Elms amongst the piles of discarded ash on 8 September 1956. Behind it is 'Merchant Navy' No 35019. No 34005 took part in the Locomotive Exchanges of 1948, working the 10.15am St Pancras–Manchester Central and 1.50pm return. *Brian Morrison*

Left: Barnstaple was the first member of the class to be rebuilt. It is seen arriving at Bournemouth Central with a down express in very dirty condition, whilst allocated to Bournemouth (71B) shed, on 22 July 1966, only three months from withdrawal. *Gavin Morrison*

21C106 *Bude*

Entered service:	4 August 1945
'Wedge' cab fitted:	May 1948
Renumbered:	34006, May 1948
BR green livery:	July 1950
Mileage (total):	1,099,338
Withdrawn:	March 1967
Fate:	Cut up Cashmores, Newport, September 1967

Above: Bude was the third member of the class to participate in the 1948 Locomotive Exchanges, working on the Western and Eastern regions. The trains involved were the 1.45pm Bristol–Plymouth and 1.35pm return the next day and the 10am Marylebone–Manchester (London Road), returning at 8.25am the next day. Excellent performances were achieved, especially on the Great Central, but with vast coal consumption. Seen here in less demanding circumstances, on 6 June 1949, No 34006 leaves Exeter St Davids with a Waterloo–Ilfracombe express, although the coaching stock would suggest otherwise. Note the 'third class' on the door of the first carriage. *Bude* achieved the highest mileage for any member of the class. *J. P. Wilson / Rail Archive Stephenson*

21C107 *Wadebridge*

Entered service:	1 September 1945
Renumbered:	34007, May 1951
BR green livery:	May 1951
'Wedge' cab fitted:	May 1951
Mileage (total):	823,193
Withdrawn:	7 October 1965
Fate:	Preserved

Right: Allocated to Salisbury shed but looking in terrible condition, No 34007 heads a Salisbury–Waterloo express through the cutting at Deepcut on 20 May 1965. *D. M. C. Hepburne-Scott / Rail Archive Stephenson*

21C108 *Padstow*

Entered service:	10 September 1945
'Wedge' cab fitted:	June 1950
Renumbered:	34008, June 1950
BR green livery:	June 1950
Mileage (unrebuilt):	597,083
Rebuilt:	July 1960
Mileage (rebuilt):	364,651
Mileage (total):	961,734
Withdrawn:	25 June 1967
Fate:	Cut up Buttigiegs, Newport, October 1967 to February 1968

Above: Looking well kept by Brighton shed, *Padstow* restarts the Brighton portion of the 1pm train from Cardiff out of Fareham on 30 April 1960. *J. C. Haydon*

Right: By now allocated to Eastleigh shed, No 34008 is ready for departure with an up train from the east end of Bournemouth Central on 1 September 1965. *Gavin Morrison*

21C109 *Lyme Regis*

Entered service:	21 September 1945
Renumbered:	34009, 22 April 1949
'Wedge' cab fitted:	December 1950
BR green livery:	December 1950
Mileage (unrebuilt):	662,481
Rebuilt:	January 1961
Mileage (rebuilt):	297,281
Mileage (total):	959,762
Withdrawn:	21 October 1966
Fate:	Cut up Buttigiegs, Newport, September 1967

Below: Allocated to Nine Elms at this time but seen on Bournemouth shed, *Lyme Regis* awaits its next duty on 24 March 1956. *C. P. Boocock*

Below: Lyme Regis appears to have received no external cleaning since being transferred to Nine Elms one month before this picture was taken of it leading a down Waterloo–Bournemouth express past Hinton Admiral in the New Forest on 23 July 1966. Signs of the third-rail electrification are evident alongside the track. *Gavin Morrison*

21C110 *Sidmouth*

Entered service:	September 1945
Renumbered:	34010, 27 January 1950
BR green livery:	January 1950
Mileage (unrebuilt):	578,944
Rebuilt:	February 1954
'Wedge' cab fitted:	February 1955
Mileage (rebuilt):	343,962
Mileage (total):	922,906
Withdrawn:	7 March 1965
Fate:	Preserved

Above: No 34010 heads an inter-regional train of Eastern stock past Lillie Bridge in North London on 8 May 1956. The engine was the last in the class to carry the temporary 'S' prefix before renumbering after Nationalisation. *J. F. Davies / Rail Archive Stephenson*

Right: A fine study of *Sidmouth*, then allocated to Nine Elms, leaving Woking and crossing to the fast road as it heads the 9.33am Waterloo–Bournemouth excursion on 3 November 1963. *Brian Stephenson*

21C111 *Tavistock*

Entered service:	October 1945
Renumbered:	34011, May 1948
BR green livery:	September 1950
'Wedge' cab fitted:	September 1952
Mileage (total):	800,455
Withdrawn:	30 November 1963
Fate:	Cut up Eastleigh Works 11 April 1964

Below: On 29 August 1963, two months after being withdrawn, *Tavistock*, still with nameplate and plaque in position, presents a sorry sight on Eastleigh, awaiting its final move to the works for scrapping. The locomotive was one of the seven members of the class to receive the experimental apple-green livery, on 26 May 1948. *Gavin Morrison*

Above right: This undated picture was probably taken when the locomotive was allocated to Plymouth Friary between April 1948 and 8 December 1950, as it is climbing Dainton Bank with an Exeter–Plymouth train. It is still in malachite green but without lettering on the tender. *Ian Allan Library*

Right: With no front numberplate or nameplate, *Launceston* presents a sorry sight as it descends the 1 in 60 of Parkstone Bank to Poole with a down Waterloo–Weymouth express on 28 July 1966. It would seem that cleaners at Bournemouth shed did not exist by this date! *Gavin Morrison*

21C112 *Launceston*

Entered service:	20 October 1945
Renumbered:	34012, 26 June 1948
'Wedge' cab fitted:	February 1951
BR green livery:	February 1951
Mileage (unrebuilt):	500,788
Rebuilt:	January 1958
Mileage (rebuilt):	346,735
Mileage (total):	847,523
Withdrawn:	11 December 1966
Fate:	Cut up Cashmores, Newport, April to June 1967

21C113 *Okehampton*

Entered service:	30 October 1945
Renumbered:	34013, 14 June 1948
BR green livery:	February 1951
'Wedge' cab fitted:	May 1954
Mileage (unrebuilt):	559,411
Rebuilt:	October 1957
Mileage (rebuilt):	385,517
Mileage (total):	944,928
Withdrawn:	9 July 1967
Fate:	Cut up Cashmores, Newport, November 1967

Above: An official picture of *Okehampton* as it entered service in October 1945, which shows the locomotive with fairing in front of its cylinders. *Ian Allan Library*

Below: A fine study of No 34013 ready to leave the west end of Basingstoke station at the head of a Waterloo–Bournemouth express on 3 January 1966. *Derek Cross*

Right: A fine portrait of *Budleigh Salterton* when only 10 months old, taken at Salisbury shed on 31 August 1946, in original condition. The locomotive spent more than 12 years allocated from new to Exmouth Junction shed. After rebuilding it was reallocated to Bricklayers Arms in London. *W. Beckerlegge / Rail Archive Stephenson*

21C114 *Budleigh Salterton*

Entered service:	12 November 1945
Renumbered:	34014, November 1948
BR green livery:	November 1949
'Wedge' cab fitted:	December 1954
Mileage (unrebuilt):	573,677
Rebuilt:	March 1958
Mileage (rebuilt):	263,800
Mileage (total):	837,477
Withdrawn:	21 March 1965
Fate:	Cut up Birds, Bridgend, May 1966

Below: Two months after being transferred to Brighton, *Budleigh Salterton* is on one of the regular duties for the class at the shed — the 11.30am Brighton–Plymouth — and is seen on the approach to Salisbury on 2 September 1962. During the seven years after rebuilding the locomotive only averaged 37,686 miles per annum. *M. J. Fox / Rail Archive Stephenson*

21C115 *Exmouth*

Entered service.	10 November 1945
Renumbered:	34015, 3 April 1948
BR green livery:	January 1950
'Wedge' cab fitted:	March 1957
Mileage (total):	903,245
Withdrawn:	16 April 1967
Fate:	Cut up Cashmores, Newport, September 1967

Below: Exmouth was allocated to either Exmouth Junction or Salisbury for its entire career, so would not have been a regular performer on Channel Island boat trains. On 31 August 1965, however, it was rostered for a down working and is pictured approaching Gas Works Junction just east of Branksome. It averaged just 42,175 miles per annum during its 21 years and five months of service. *Gavin Morrison*

Right: An unusual viewpoint in August 1947 of *Bodmin* giving the up 'Devon Belle' banking assistance out of Ilfracombe up the almost continuous gradient of 1 in 36 to Mortehoe three miles away. It spent the first 12½ years of its career at Exmouth Junction before rebuilding. *C. A. Todhunter*

Below: After rebuilding in April 1958 *Bodmin* moved to Ramsgate shed, which is probably why it was selected for this special duty of hauling the train conveying the Italian President from Dover to London (Victoria) on 13 May 1958. It is seen at the head of the train at Bickley. Since preservation, No 34016 has been one of the two rebuilt 'West Country' class to work on the national network. As an unrebuilt engine it averaged 44,636 miles per annum and, as a rebuild, it achieved virtually the same annual average.
John Head / Rail Archive Stephenson

21C116 *Bodmin*	
Entered service:	28 November 1945
Renumbered:	34016, 3 July 1948
BR green livery:	January 1950
'Wedge' cab fitted:	May 1953
Mileage (unrebuilt):	554,230
Rebuilt:	April 1958
Mileage (rebuilt):	257,444
Mileage (total):	811,674
Withdrawn:	14 June 1964
Fate:	Preserved

Right: After nine years from new at Exmouth Junction *Ilfracombe* was reallocated to Stewarts Lane. In severe winter weather conditions, which frequently happen in Kent, it is recorded heading the 11.35am Victoria–Ramsgate express through Bickley in February 1955. *S. Creer*

Below: During its second period allocated to Bricklayers Arms between 14 June 1959 and 17 January 1961, *Ilfracombe* is pictured working the up 'Man of Kent' near Orpington in May 1960. It then returned to the South Western Division where it remained until withdrawn. *Derek Cross*

21C117 *Ilfracombe*

Entered service:	8 December 1945
Renumbered:	34017, 29 May 1948
BR green livery:	January 1951
'Wedge' cab fitted:	January 1954
Mileage (unrebuilt):	459,309
Rebuilt:	November 1957
Mileage (rebuilt):	397,332
Mileage (total):	856,641
Withdrawn:	2 October 1966
Fate:	Cut up Buttigiegs, Newport, October 1967 to February 1968

Below: No 34017 heads an up express from Bournemouth West in the woods to the west of Bournemouth Central on 23 July 1966, one month after being reallocated to Nine Elms from Eastleigh. *Gavin Morrison*

21C118 *Axminster*

Entered service:	17 December 1945
Renumbered:	34018, June 1948
'Wedge' cab fitted:	October 1950
BR green livery:	October 1950
Mileage (unrebuilt):	547,303
Rebuilt:	September 1958
Mileage (rebuilt):	427,014
Mileage (total):	974,317
Withdrawn:	9 July 1967
Fate:	Cut up Cashmores, Newport, April 1968

Above: A picture taken before 11 April 1951 as *Axminster* was transferred away from Exmouth Junction to Nine Elms on this date and it is still carrying the 72A shed code. It is shown on Yeovil Junction shed. *Rail Archive Stephenson*

Right: Nine Elms's cleaners must have been busy on *Axminster* before it worked the down 'Bournemouth Belle' on 24 March 1963. It is shown at Deepcut. *D. M. C. Hepburne-Scott / Rail Archive Stephenson*

Below: A fine panoramic view of *Axminster* as it approaches Clapham Junction at the head of a Waterloo–Bournemouth express in September 1965. *Brian Stephenson*

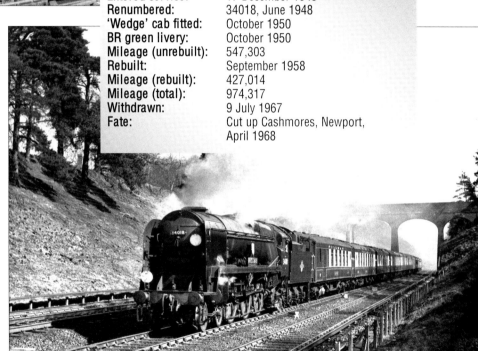

21C119 *Bideford*

Entered service:	21 December 1945
Renumbered:	34019, May 1948
BR green livery:	November 1949
'Wedge' cab fitted:	January 1956
Mileage (total):	701,316
Withdrawn:	19 March 1967
Fate:	Cut up Cashmores, Newport, September 1967

Below: No 21C119 attracts a crowd at Victoria as it waits to leave on the down 'Golden Arrow' sometime before 29 August 1946 when it received its name, which is absent in this picture. It is strange that it should be on this duty at this time as it was allocated to Exmouth Junction until April 1948. *Bideford* was one of two members of the class to be converted to oil burning with a single burner in July 1947. It did not work well with one burner and was altered to two later. It returned to coal firing in September 1948. *C. R. L. Coles / Rail Archive Stephenson*

21C120 *Seaton*

Entered service:	31 December 1945
Renumbered:	34020, May 1948
'Wedge' cab fitted:	July 1950
BR green livery:	July 1950
Mileage (total):	789,698
Withdrawn:	September 1964
Fate:	Cut up Birds, Swansea, December 1964

Below: Coasting down the bank off Battledown Flyover past Worting Junction during March 1960, *Seaton* is probably slowing for a stop at Basingstoke. At the time it was allocated to Nine Elms; the only other shed it was based at during its career was Exmouth Junction. *Derek Cross*

Left: Dartmoor pictured on one of the centre roads at Exeter Central station on 14 August 1952, before the 'wedge' cab was fitted. It was allocated to Exmouth Junction at this time. *R. O. Tuck / Rail Archive Stephenson*

21C121 *Dartmoor*

Entered service:	18 January 1946
Renumbered:	34021, 10 July 1948
BR green livery:	June 1950
'Wedge' cab fitted:	July 1953
Mileage (unrebuilt):	541,097
Rebuilt:	December 1957
Mileage (rebuilt):	409,045
Mileage (total):	950,142
Withdrawn:	9 July 1967
Fate:	Cut up Cashmores, Newport, March 1968

Below: Devoid of its nameplate, *Dartmoor* blows off as it coasts round the long sweeping curve at the top of Poole Harbour past Holes Bay, junction with the ex-Somerset & Dorset Joint, with the Weymouth portion of an up Waterloo express on 7 September 1965. The stock illustrated here would be combined at Bournemouth Central with coaches from Bournemouth West. *Gavin Morrison*

Right: Allocated to Exmouth Junction when this picture was taken on 2 July 1954, *Exmoor* leaves Salisbury with a Waterloo–Plymouth express. *Brian Morrison*

Below: Exmoor was reallocated to Eastleigh on 26 May 1961 where it remained until withdrawn. Seen in fine external condition, the locomotive is at the head of a Waterloo–Exeter express near Oakley on 18 September 1961. *Rail Archive Stephenson*

21C122 *Exmoor*

Entered service:	25 January 1946
Renumbered:	34022, 12 June 1948
BR green livery:	September 1950
'Wedge' cab fitted:	April 1953
Mileage (unrebuilt):	527,822
Rebuilt:	December 1959
Mileage (rebuilt):	265,825
Mileage (total):	793,647
Withdrawn:	25 April 1965
Fate:	Cut up Woodfield, Newport, August 1965

21C123 *Blackmore Vale*

Entered service:	4 February 1946
Renumbered:	34023, 17 April 1948
BR green livery:	April 1950
'Wedge' cab fitted:	October 1954
Mileage (total):	921,268
Withdrawn:	9 July 1967
Fate:	Preserved
Note:	Named *Blackmoor Vale* until April 1950

Below: Blackmoor Vale was a popular locomotive on railtours towards the end of steam on the Southern Region and, since preservation, has become one of the best-known members of the class. It achieved 21 years five months of service, the third longest for an unrebuilt member of the class. Here it is seen in terrible external condition, whilst allocated to Eastleigh, rushing past Basingstoke with an up express on 24 September 1966. *Gavin Morrison*

21C124 *Tamar Valley*

Entered service:	11 February 1946
Renumbered:	34024, 26 June 1948
BR green livery:	December 1951
'Wedge' cab fitted:	March 1955
Mileage (unrebuilt):	689,964
Rebuilt:	February 1961
Mileage (rebuilt):	150,000
Mileage (total):	839,964
Withdrawn:	9 July 1967
Fate:	Cut up Cashmores, Newport, March to September 1968

Left: Class E1/R 0-6-0T No 32124 is on shunting duties in the yard at the top of the 1 in 37 bank into Exeter Central from St David's, as a very dirty *Tamar Valley* passes with four coaches on an Ilfracombe–Exeter Central train on 29 May 1956. Both locomotives were allocated to Exmouth Junction shed. *J. P. Wilson / Rail Archive Stephenson*

Left: Tamar Valley seems to be struggling to lift this inter-regional express up the 1 in 176 bank across Brockenhurst Common after a stop at Brockenhurst station on 19 April 1965. The locomotive had the dubious distinction of achieving by far the lowest mileage of a rebuild, only covering 150,000 miles during its six-year five-month career. By comparison No 34096, in only three years five months as a rebuild, managed 211,046 miles. *Gavin Morrison*

Right: Super power for a portion of the down 'Atlantic Coast Express' as *Whimple* pilots another member of the class out of Exeter St Davids on 27 June 1952.
W.S. Garth / Rail Archive Stephenson

Below: Whimple is pictured at its then home shed of Eastleigh under repair on 9 September 1965. It ran in rebuilt form for nine years eight months and, along with No 34001, was the second-longest-serving rebuild, although the mileages covered were very different: No 34001 covered 495,163, whereas No 34025 managed just 360,454.
Gavin Morrison

21C125 *Whimple*

Entered service:	4 March 1946
Renumbered:	34025, 2 October 1948
BR green livery:	March 1950
'Wedge' cab fitted:	September 1954
Mileage (unrebuilt):	512,484
Rebuilt:	October 1957
Mileage (rebuilt):	360,454
Mileage (total):	872,938
Withdrawn:	9 July 1967
Fate:	Cut up Cashmores, Newport, March 1968
Note:	Named *Rough Tor* between 11-23 April 1948, to *Whimple* 3 May 1948

Left: No 34026 is recorded leaving the east end of Exeter St Davids with probably the Ilfracombe portion of an express from Waterloo on 27 June 1952.
It was, on 14 October 1955, the last member of the class to be named.
*W. S. Garth /
Rail Archive Stephenson*

21C126 *Yes Tor*

Entered service:	6 April 1946
'Wedge' cab fitted:	May 1949
Renumbered:	34026, 27 May 1949
BR green livery:	December 1950
Mileage (unrebuilt):	563,491
Rebuilt:	February 1958
Mileage (rebuilt):	352,753
Mileage (total):	916,244
Withdrawn:	18 September 1966
Fate:	Cut up Buttigiegs, Newport, 5 October 1967

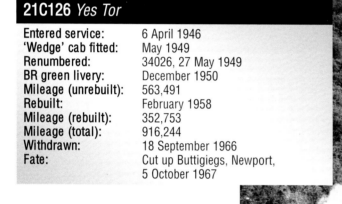

Right: During its 16 months' allocation to Ramsgate shed, *Yes Tor* is seen in June 1959 heading a train for Victoria through Folkestone Warren, with the White Cliffs in the background.
Derek Cross

Left: Devoid of its nameplate but commendably clean, *Yes Tor,* after a non-classified visit to the works, is pictured on Eastleigh shed on 14 November 1965.
John Vaughan

21C127 *Taw Valley*

Entered service:	15 April 1946
Renumbered:	34027, 3 July 1948
BR green livery:	December 1950
'Wedge' cab fitted:	June 1953
Mileage (unrebuilt):	503,085
Rebuilt:	September 1957
Mileage (rebuilt):	261,231
Mileage (total):	764,316
Withdrawn:	9 August 1964
Fate:	Preserved

Above: Leaning on the curve and shut-off, *Taw Valley* passes under Battledown Flyover at the head of a Plymouth–Waterloo express on 8 September 1952 during the period of nine years eight months it spent allocated to Exmouth Junction shed. *Brian Morrison*

Right: Taw Valley is seen heading past Knockholt during May 1959 at the head of a Victoria-Dover-Ramsgate express. As with No 34016 *Bodmin*, No 34027 has travelled extensively on the national network since being preserved and has appeared sometimes in a red livery in connection with the filming of the Harry Potter novels. *Derek Cross*

21C128 *Eddystone*

Entered service:	1 May 1946
Renumbered:	34028, 18 December 1948
BR green livery:	December 1951
'Wedge' cab fitted:	February 1954
Mileage (unrebuilt):	564,587
Rebuilt:	August 1958
Mileage (rebuilt):	286,962
Mileage (total):	851,549
Withdrawn:	31 May 1964
Fate:	Preserved

Left: This picture is undated, but it will probably be 1946 as the locomotive is still unnamed.
No 21C128 went new to Ramsgate for 21 months before moving to the West Country. It is shown heading through Tonbridge. *H. C. Casserley*

Right: Light work for *Eddystone*, as was often the case for the Exmouth Junction-allocated Light Pacifics, as it pauses at Seaton Junction with an up local train from Exeter Central on 3 July 1956. *Hugh Ballantyne*

Below: One month after rebuilding *Eddystone* is heading for the ash pits on Nine Elms shed on 13 September 1958. Now restored from ex-Barry condition, the locomotive is currently working in preservation. *Gavin Morrison*

21C129 *Lundy*

Entered service:	13 May 1946
Renumbered:	34029, 12 February 1949
BR green livery:	February 1951
'Wedge' cab fitted:	January 1955
Mileage (unrebuilt):	580,259
Rebuilt:	December 1958
Mileage (rebuilt):	248,230
Mileage (total):	828,489
Withdrawn:	13 September 1964
Fate:	Cut up Woods, Queenborough, February 1965

Above right: When only one month old and unnamed, No 21C129 is seen as built on Stewarts Lane shed; the locomotive was allocated to Ramsgate on 15 June 1946. *H. C. Casserley*

Right: After working a schools' special over the Somerset & Dorset line, piloted by BR Standard Class 4MT No 75007, *Lundy* is being coaled at Bath Green Park shed ready for the return working. The year is believed to be 1960. *Rail Photoprints*

Below: Lundy departs Southampton without a trace of exhaust on a hot summer's day in June 1960. *Derek Cross*

Above: Watersmeet is approaching Wilton at the head of the 3.35pm service from Waterloo to Yeovil Town on 3 August 1964. *M. Mensing*

Below: At 7.30pm *Watersmeet* heads an up fitted container train off the Southern line at Cowley Bridge Junction, Exeter, on 14 June 1959. *M. Mensing*

21C130 *Watersmeet*

Entered service:	20 May 1946
Renumbered:	34030, 20 November 1948
'Wedge' cab fitted:	January 1952
BR green livery:	March 1952
Mileage (total):	744,279
Withdrawn:	September 1964
Fate:	Cut up Birds, Swansea, 1964

Right: A very dirty *Torrington* pulls away from Salisbury at the head of the 5pm service from Waterloo to Yeovil on 12 May 1958. *Brian Morrison*

Below: The fireman on *Torrington* has come across to have a look at the 'Lord Nelson' heading a Bournemouth–Waterloo service, as the 'West Country' overtakes it between Basingstoke and Worting Junction with train from Weymouth in July 1960. *Derek Cross*

21C131 *Torrington*

Entered service:	30 June 1946
Renumbered:	34031, 29 January 1949
'Wedge' cab fitted:	January 1949
BR green livery:	November 1949
Mileage (unrebuilt):	552,594
Rebuilt:	November 1958
Mileage (rebuilt):	288,588
Mileage (total):	841,182
Withdrawn:	7 February 1965
Fate:	Cut up Cashmores, Newport, May 1965

21C132 *Camelford*

Entered service:	18 June 1946
Renumbered:	34032, 10 April 1948
'Wedge' cab fitted:	January 1951
BR green livery:	January 1951
Mileage (unrebuilt):	649,155
Rebuilt:	October 1960
Mileage (rebuilt):	204,243
Mileage (total):	853,398
Withdrawn:	2 October 1966
Fate:	Cut up Buttigiegs, Newport, betweeen May and October 1967

Above: Ten days after being renumbered 34032 and with 'BRITISH RAILWAYS' lettering on the tender, *Camelford* makes a fine sight in malachite-green livery as it heads an up express towards Winchfield, having just overtaken a train on the up slow on 20 April 1948. *E. C. Griffith / Rail Archive Stephenson*

Below: Travelling at speed, *Camelford* approaches Basingstoke with a down express for Bournemouth on 24 September 1966. The locomotive is looking in good external condition considering it was withdrawn one month later from Salisbury shed. *Gavin Morrison*

Right: Out on the 'withered arm' of the LSWR in Cornwall *Chard* leaves Delabole at the head of an up local freight on the Wadebridge–Launceston line on 3 June 1957. *Weatherill / Rail Archive Stephenson*

21C133 *Chard*

Entered service:	29 June 1946
Renumbered:	34033, 10 December 48
'Wedge' cab fitted:	June 1949
BR green livery:	December 1951
Mileage (total):	884,916
Withdrawn:	19 December 1965
Fate:	Cut up Buttigiegs, Newport, May 1966

21C134 *Honiton*

Entered service:	11 July 1946
Renumbered:	34034, 2 July 1948
BR green livery:	May 1950
'Wedge' cab fitted:	April 1955
Mileage (unrebuilt):	636,999
Rebuilt:	August 1960
Mileage (rebuilt):	305,134
Mileage (total):	942,133
Withdrawn:	2 July 1967
Fate:	Cut up Buttigiegs, Newport, April 1968

Right: No 21C134 is recorded in unpainted condition outside Brighton Works, although the tender has been completed, before entering service on 11 July 1946. *Ian Allan Library*

Below: A powerful silhouette of *Honiton* as it heads west near Redbridge, with Southampton Water in the background, in 1966. *John Vaughan*

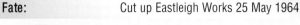

21C135 *Shaftesbury*

Entered service:	July 1946
Renumbered:	34035, January 1949
'Wedge' cab fitted:	February 1952
BR green livery:	February 1952
Mileage (total):	764,306
Withdrawn:	8 June 1963
Fate:	Cut up Eastleigh Works 25 May 1964

Left: Shaftesbury was among the first batch of four in the class to be withdrawn. In an attempt to solve the problem of drifting smoke it was modified with deflectors that curved in and continued in one piece across the top. This modification was undertaken in 1960 and it was not pursued on any other locomotives. As with the 'Merchant Navy' class, the problem of smoke drifting was never sorted out on the unrebuilt Light Pacifics. In September 1959, before the modification, No 34035 is shown at Sidmouth Junction on an Exeter–Yeovil pick-up goods. *Derek Cross*

Below: Shaftesbury was transferred seven times in its first four-and-a-half years until it moved to Plymouth Friary on 8 December 1950, where it stayed just over seven years. Seen during this period, it is entering Exeter St Davids with a train from Plymouth on 23 June 1952. *W. S. Garth / Rail Archive Stephenson*

21C136 _Westward Ho_	
Entered service:	29 July 1946
Renumbered:	34036, 22 May 1948
'Wedge' cab fitted:	February 1952
BR green livery:	February 1952
Mileage (unrebuilt):	582,544
Rebuilt:	August 1960
Mileage (rebuilt):	312,002
Mileage (total):	894,546
Withdrawn:	9 July 1967
Fate:	Cut up Cashmores, Newport, February 1968

Above: Still unnamed, No 34036 enters St Budeaux Victoria Road with an Exeter–Plymouth Friary stopping train in April 1951. Note that the locomotive is still in malachite green but with the BR lion-and-wheel emblem; only three other members of the class ran in this condition. Along with _Bideford_ (No 34019) this locomotive was converted to oil-burning in February 1948. Although both eventually performed very well following this conversion, No 34036 reverted to coal in 1949. _W. J. V. Anderson / Rail Archive Stephenson_

Right: Now named _Westward Ho_, No 34036 is shown at Gillingham with the 12.48pm local from Templecombe to Salisbury on 21 August 1958. _Hugh Ballantyne_

Above: Westward Ho is seen ex-works after rebuilding on Eastleigh shed awaiting its return to traffic on 11 September 1960. *Gavin Morrison*

Left: Whilst allocated to Eastleigh, *Westward Ho* is shown passing Reading West with the 10.8am York–Bournemouth working on 3 April 1965. *Brian Stephenson*

Below: Another view of *Westward Ho*, this time heading an up express through the New Forest near Hinton Admiral, one month after being transferred to Nine Elms shed, on 23 July 1966. *Gavin Morrison*

Left: When new, unnamed No 21C137, whilst allocated to Stewarts Lane shed, is shown at St Mary Cray Junction at the head of a forces' leave special in the autumn of 1946.
Rail Archive Stephenson

21C137 *Clovelly*

Entered service:	30 August 1946
Renumbered:	34037, 25 March 1949
'Wedge' cab fitted:	March 1949
BR green livery:	October 1950
Mileage (unrebuilt):	480,115
Rebuilt:	March 1958
Mileage (rebuilt):	330543
Mileage (total):	810,658
Withdrawn:	9 July 1967
Fate:	Cut up Cashmores, Newport, March 1968

Left: Now allocated to Nine Elms shed, *Clovelly* is pictured ready to leave Basingstoke with a train for Bournemouth on 24 September 1966. *Gavin Morrison*

21C138 *Lynton*

Entered service:	5 September 1946
Renumbered:	34038, 12 February 1949
BR green livery:	May 1952
'Wedge' cab fitted:	April 1955
Mileage (total):	819,984
Withdrawn:	12 June 1967
Fate:	Cut up Cashmores, Newport, September 1966

Right: Lynton heading a down Waterloo–Exeter relief near Brookwood in September 1960 during its time allocated to Exmouth Junction shed.
Derek Cross

21C139 *Boscastle*

Entered service:	16 September 1946
Renumbered:	34039, 18 June 1948
BR green livery:	August 1949
'Wedge' cab fitted:	November 1952
Mileage (unrebuilt):	466,238
Rebuilt:	January 1959
Mileage (rebuilt):	279,270
Mileage (total):	745,508
Withdrawn:	9 May 1965
Fate:	Preserved

Right: Initially shedded at Stewarts Lane No 34039 is photographed on an unrecorded working taken shortly after Nationalisation and with the front numberplate but no tender lettering. *E. R. Wethersett*

Left: A powerful picture of *Boscastle* leaving Liverpool Street with a holiday campers' special in 1951. No 34039 was the first of the class to be painted in BR Brunswick green. On 27 April 1949 No 34059 went to the Great Eastern on trial and returned to the Southern by 30 May 1949. Whilst on the ER the locomotive was liked by some crews and not by others. On 8 May 1951 No 34039 was sent, to be followed by Nos 34057/65/76/89, and during its stay *Boscastle* got as far north as Doncaster, on 16 July 1951. Whilst the five SR locomotives were on the Great Eastern, the then new 'Britannia' class Pacifics were taken out of traffic as a result of mechanical problems. By May 1952 all five of the Bulleid Light Pacifics had returned to the Southern Region. *F. R. Hebron / Rail Archive Stephenson*

Left: The external condition of *Boscastle* does credit to its home shed of Eastleigh in this view dated 9 June 1963. The locomotive is heading an up Waterloo express past Bournemouth West Junction. In the background can be seen the extensive carriage sidings, which later became the site of the EMU depot. Bournemouth West station closed on 4 October 1965. *Gavin Morrison*

21C140 Crewkerne

Entered service:	23 September 1946
Renumbered:	34040, 15 October 1948
BR green livery:	August 1950
'Wedge' cab fitted:	March 1954
Mileage (unrebuilt):	500,397
Rebuilt:	October 1960
Mileage (rebuilt):	269,227
Mileage (total):	769,624
Withdrawn:	2 July 1967
Fate:	Cut up Cashmores, Newport, March 1968

Below: A few months before rebuilding, *Crewkerne* is pictured on its home shed at Bournemouth on 21 February 1960. Previously it had been allocated to Bath Green Park on two occasions in the early 1950s for Somerset & Dorset duties. *Ian Allan Library*

Below: Seen in fine external condition whilst allocated to Bournemouth shed, *Crewkerne* waits on the ash pits at Nine Elms shed for servicing on 8 April 1964. *Gavin Morrison*

21C141 Wilton

Entered service:	30 September 1946
Renumbered:	34041, 29 January 1949
BR green livery:	June 1951
'Wedge' cab fitted:	December 1950
Mileage (total):	626,417
Withdrawn:	23 January 1966
Fate:	Cut up Cashmores, Newport, January 1966

Left: Wilton achieved the second lowest annual mileage of only 32,451 miles during its career of 19 years three months. This may be due to the fact that it spent three-and-a half years working mainly on the S&D line. Here we see it at Bath Green Park awaiting departure on the 7.5pm to Bournemouth West, which was the last through train of the day, on 29 May 1963. *Hugh Ballantyne*

Left: Piloted on 9 September 1961 by long-time S&D-allocated '2P' 4-4-0 No 40634, *Wilton* pauses at Shepton Mallet on a Bournemouth West-Liverpool summer Saturdays extra, before tackling the 3½ miles at 1 in 50 to Masbury Summit. The Somerset & Dorset line closed on 7 March 1966. *Gavin Morrison*

21C142 Dorchester

Entered service:	7 October 1946
Renumbered:	34042, 5 June 1948
'Wedge' cab fitted:	April 1949
BR green livery:	November 1951
Mileage (unrebuilt):	477,413
Rebuilt:	January 1959
Mileage (rebuilt):	249,348
Mileage (total):	726,761
Withdrawn:	3 October 1965
Fate:	Cut up Buttigiegs, Newport, April 1966

Right Well cleaned by Eastleigh shed, *Dorchester* heads an up express near Sway on 17 June 1955.
D. M. C. Hepburne-Scott / Rail Archive Stephenson

Right Although not actually transferred to Eastleigh until 14 September 1964, *Dorchester* had already arrived by the 12th when this picture was taken of it on the shed. *Gavin Morrison*

21C143 *Combe Martin*

Entered service:	15 October 1946
Renumbered:	34043, 18 September 1948
BR green livery:	September 1950
'Wedge' cab fitted:	June 1952
Mileage (total):	749,112
Withdrawn:	8 June 1963
Fate:	Cut up Eastleigh Works 21 September 1963

Left: Allocated to Bournemouth for over 11 years, *Combe Martin* was eventually amongst the first batch of the class to be withdrawn in 1963. It is seen here leaving Bath Green Park on 29 August 1959 with the 'Pines Express' from Manchester London Road to Bournemouth West. Note the tablet-catcher for the single-line tablet to be taken at Bath Junction box and the unique S&D headcode. *Hugh Ballantyne*

Left: Another view of *Combe Martin* on S&D duties, this time being piloted by ex-LMS '2P' No 40697 as it heads a summer Saturdays Bournemouth West–Manchester London Road service past Masbury Halt on 12 August 1961. The station closed with the line on 7 March 1966. *Gavin Morrison*

21C144 *Woollacombe*

Entered service:	22 October 1946
Renumbered:	34044, 1 January 1949
BR green livery:	December 1950
'Wedge' cab fitted:	March 1954
Mileage (unrebuilt):	571,638
Rebuilt:	May 1960
Mileage (rebuilt):	323,360
Mileage (total):	894,998
Withdrawn:	21 May 1967
Fate:	Cut up Cashmores, Newport, September 1967

Above: An interesting picture of *Woolacombe* passing Hove *en route* to Brighton on 12 May 1956 towing 'King Arthur' No 30740 *Merlin*, which had been at the Longmoor Military Railway to be filmed in a staged collision. *W. M. J. Jackson*

Left: Pictured during the period of almost when it was 15 years it was allocated to Bournemouth shed, *Woolacombe* is seen at Southampton with an up Bournemouth–Waterloo working on 3 January 1966. *Derek Cross*

Above: Fresh from a general overhaul, *Ottery St Mary* makes a fine sight on Eastleigh shed before returning to traffic on 16 June 1957. Note it retains the side raves on the tender with the final BR emblem. It achieved almost equal annual figures in unrebuilt and rebuilt form, averaging around 43,000 miles per annum.
J. F. Davies / Rail Archive Stephenson

Right: Ottery St Mary has just arrived at Evercreech Junction with a summer Saturday train from Bournemouth West to Manchester and Liverpool on 12 August 1961. Ex-S&D 4-4-0 No 40634 stands in the centre road waiting to join as pilot for the trip over the Mendips.
Gavin Morrison

21C146 *Braunton*

Entered service:	16 November 1946
Renumbered:	34046, 22 January 1949
BR green livery:	August 1950
'Wedge' cab fitted:	January 1954
Mileage (unrebuilt):	515,391
Rebuilt:	February 1954
Mileage (rebuilt):	263,819
Mileage (total):	779,210
Withdrawn:	10 October 1965
Fate:	Preserved

Above: An interesting comparison of front-end numbering: on the right is *Budleigh Salterton* in original condition whilst on the left is *Braunton* showing both 34046 and s21C146. There were 22 locomotives that received the 's' prefix. The picture was taken at Exmouth Junction on 7 April 1949. *A. J. Cook*

Below: Braunton spent around 7½ years allocated to Brighton as an unrebuilt locomotive. This picture is believed to have been taken at Riddlesdown, near Sanderstead, between 1951 and 1959. *Rail Photoprints collection*

Above: After rebuilding in February 1959 *Braunton* was selected to work the royal train between Weymouth and Southampton in April of that year. Its external condition on that occasion would surely have been different from that shown in this picture of it leaving Southampton at the head of another prestigious train — the 'Bournemouth Belle' — on 5 October 1965. *Derek Cross*

Right: Braunton is seen on its home shed of Bournemouth on 8 September 1965. *Gavin Morrison*

Right: In rebuilt form and working the S&D, No 34046, piloted by local BR Standard Class 5MT No 73051, climbs the 1 in 50 out of Bath to Devonshire Tunnel with the 'Pines Express' on 23 April 1962. *Gavin Morrison*

21C147 *Callington*

Entered service:	23 November 1946
Renumbered:	34047, 18 January 1949
BR green livery:	December 1951
'Wedge' cab fitted:	September 1953
Mileage (unrebuilt):	513,822
Rebuilt:	November 1958
Mileage (rebuilt):	332,169
Mileage (total):	845,991
Withdrawn:	25 June 1967
Fate:	Cut up Buttigiegs, Newport, October 1967 to February 1968

Above: A very interesting picture at the unusual location of Bristol Bath Road shows *Callington* and classmate No 34048 *Crediton* alongside ex-Great Western locomotives on 20 March 1954. The reason for the presence of the two 'West Country' class locomotives is not recorded on the photograph, but it could have been due to problems with the 'Kings' and 'Britannias' around this time. *Rail Photoprints*

Below: Seen from Battersea Rise, *Callington* nears the end of its journey as it approaches Clapham Junction with an up Sunday morning train from Bournemouth in April 1965. *Brian Stephenson*

Right: Shortly after Nationalisation, *Crediton* is seen at Exeter Central. *Ian Allan Library*

Below right: Nameplate, crest and scroll as fited to No 34048 *Crediton*. *Brian Stephenson*

Below: A fine study of *Crediton* on 14 April 1960 as it approaches Honiton Tunnel with a Waterloo–Exeter express during the period when it was allocated to Salisbury shed. No 34048 is still carrying the shedplate for Bournemouth, from where it had been transferred one month earlier. *D. M. C. Hepburne-Scott / Rail Archive Stephenson*

21C148 *Crediton*

Entered service:	30 November 1946
Renumbered:	34048, 21 August 1948
'Wedge' cab fitted:	May 1949
BR green livery:	August 1952
Mileage (unrebuilt):	539,988
Rebuilt:	14 March 1959
Mileage (rebuilt):	307,627
Mileage (total):	847,615
Withdrawn:	13 March 1966
Fate:	Cut up Cashmores, Newport, July 1966

21C149 *Anti-Aircraft Command*

Entered service:	9 December 1946
Renumbered:	34049, 1 April 1949
'Wedge' cab fitted:	March 1948
BR green livery:	June 1951
Mileage (total):	723,947
Withdrawn:	7 December 1963
Fate:	Cut up Eastleigh Works 6 June 1964

Above: Anti-Aircraft Command, the first of the 'Battle of Britain' locomotives, is seen eight months after Nationalisation on 28 August 1948 with 'British Railways' on the tender and the 's' prefix. No 21C149 was one of the 22 locomotives to receive the latter. It is working a Brighton–Exeter express at Semley on 28 August 1948 when allocated to Salisbury. As the class was going to be working in the southeast for several years, it was decided that West Country names were not suitable and Battle of Britain personalities, squadrons and aircraft were selected as an alternative. As it turned out, *Anti-Aircraft Command* went new to Salisbury and spent its entire career allocated to South Western Division sheds. Along with No 34035 it was selected for experiments aimed at solving the problem of drifting smoke; as part of these No 34049 had its smoke-defelctors removed altogether, although these would be restored by February 1960. *A. C. Cawston*

21C150 *Royal Observer Corps*

Entered service:	16 December 1946
Renumbered:	34050, 29 January 1949
'Wedge' cab fitted:	February 1948
BR green livery:	April 1952
Mileage (unrebuilt):	509,320
Rebuilt:	August 1958
Mileage (rebuilt):	287,494
Mileage (total):	796,814
Withdrawn:	29 August 1965
Fate:	Cut up Birds, Swansea, December 1965

Above: A very fine study of *Royal Observer Corps* as it heads a down West of England express from Waterloo near Winchfield on 29 April 1949. It was a Salisbury-allocated locomotive at the time and only spent one year of its career on the South Eastern Division.
E. C. Griffith / Rail Archive Stephenson

Right: Illustrating the impressive plaque and nameplate fitted to the locomotive, with the plates on the cabside showing medal ribbons, *Royal Observer Corps* is pictured on Salisbury shed during the period it was allocated to Nine Elms. This picture, taken on 23 April 1962, shows the 9ft wide 5,500gal tender to advantage.
Gavin Morrison

21C151 *Winston Churchill*

Entered service:	30 December 1946
Renumbered:	34051, 23 October 1948
'Wedge' cab fitted:	August 1947
BR green livery:	December 1950
Mileage (total):	807,496
Withdrawn:	19 September 1965
Fate:	Preserved

Above left: The nameplate from No 34051 *Winston Churchill*. Note how the class name was incorporated on the plate *Brian Stephenson*

Above: Until its naming by Lord Dowding at Waterloo on 11 September 1947 No 21C151 had been just another member of the class. It then became the best-known member after being named *Winston Churchill*. It had been hoped the great man would have been present at the ceremony, but this was not to be, and so Lord Dowding did the honours for both Nos 21C151 and 21C152. The locomotive is shown hauling Winston Churchill's funeral train past Virginia Water on its journey from Waterloo to Handborough on 30 January 1965. No 34051 is now in the National Collection. *Brian Stephenson*

Centre left: Seen after withdrawal, *Winston Churchill* is recorded at the very unlikely location of Leeds Holbeck shed on 10 December 1965 whilst in transit to Hellifield shed for safe storage. *Gavin Morrison*

Left: Winston Churchill is seen on Bournemouth shed on 28 October 1962. This was another 'Battle of Britain' never to be allocated to the South Eastern Division, spending around 17 years at Salisbury. *Gavin Morrison*

21C152 Lord Dowding

Entered service:	31 December 1946
Renumbered:	34052, 19 February 1949
'Wedge' cab fitted:	August 1947
BR green livery:	August 1952
Mileage (unrebuilt):	507,986
Rebuilt:	September 1958
Mileage (rebuilt):	428,516
Mileage (total):	936,502
Withdrawn:	9 July 1967
Fate:	Cut up Cashmores, Newport, February 1968

Left: Lord Dowding approaches Seaton Junction with an up Exmouth–Waterloo train on 9 July 1949. *H. C. Casserley*

Below: A panoramic view of Waterloo, recorded from a nearby block of flats on 26 August 1966, features *Lord Dowding* leaving with the 6pm service to Salisbury as Standard 2-6-4T No 80012 arrives with empty stock. *Brian Stephenson*

21C153 Sir Keith Park

Entered service:	21 January 1947
'Wedge' cab fitted:	August 1947
Renumbered:	34053, 10 June 1949
BR green livery:	January 1951
Mileage (unrebuilt):	529,129
Rebuilt:	November 1958
Mileage (rebuilt):	296,188
Mileage (total):	825,317
Withdrawn:	17 October 1965
Fate:	Preserved

Above: A fine picture of
No 21C153 after being named
by Sir Keith Park at Brighton
on 19 September 1947.
W. Beckerlegge /
Rail Archive Stephenson

Above: In fine external condition,
No 34053 arrives at Exeter St Davids
on 27 June 1952 with a heavy ballast
train from Meldon Quarry. It will
attach a pilot and probably two
bankers to assist it up the 1-in-37
climb to Exeter Central.
W. S. Garth /
Rail Archive Stephenson

Left: Sir Keith Park recorded at the
head of some empty stock facing
west on the now removed centre
road at Bournemouth Central
on 1 September 1965. It was
withdrawn six weeks later.
Gavin Morrison

21C154 *Lord Beaverbrook*

Entered service:	January 1947
'Wedge' cab fitted:	September 1947
Renumbered:	34054, March 1949
BR green livery:	April 1951
Mileage (total):	737,443
Withdrawn:	September 1964
Fate:	Cut up Birds, Bynea, March 1965

Below: Named by Lord Beaverbrook at Waterloo on 16 September 1947, No 34054 is shown at the head of a ballast train from Meldon Quarry at Sidmouth Junction in May 1956.
Weatherill / Rail Archive Stephenson

Right: On 17 August 1961 No 34055 is pictured on Eastleigh shed awaiting a visit to the works for its last general repair. It was named *Fighter Pilot* at Brighton, appropriately by Group Captain Douglas Bader, on 19 September 1947. It was also the last member of the class to be repainted in malachite green and subsequently was one of the first batch of withdrawals. *Gavin Morrison*

21C155 *Fighter Pilot*

Entered service:	13 February 1947
'Wedge' cab fitted:	September 1947
Renumbered:	34055, 22 July 1949
BR green livery:	May 1951
Mileage (total):	706,607
Withdrawn:	22 June 1963
Fate:	Cut up Eastleigh Works 2 May 1964

Right: Fighter Pilot makes a spectacular departure from Brighton with a train for Plymouth in March 1961. *Brian Haresnape*

21C156 *Croydon*

Entered service:	25 February 1947
'Wedge' cab fitted:	November 1947
Renumbered:	34056, 29 May 1948
BR green livery:	January 1950
Mileage (unrebuilt):	634,179
Rebuilt:	December 1960
Mileage (rebuilt):	322,902
Mileage (total):	957,081
Withdrawn:	7 May 1967
Fate:	Cut up Cashmores, Newport, September 1967

Left:
Allocated to Dover, *Croydon*, in immaculate condition, heads the up 'Night Ferry' past Sevenoaks during May 1948. *A. W. Croughton / Rail Archive Stephenson*

Right: No 34056 was one of seven members of the class to receive an experimental BR apple-green livery, in which it operated from 3 June 1948 until 19 January 1950. Complete with 'BRITISH RAILWAYS' on the tender, the locomotive is seen here in the apple-green livery heading a heavy Continental boat train, probably during the second half of 1949 when it was allocated to Stewarts Lane shed. *E. R. Wethersett*

Left: No 34056 on shed at Salisbury on 23 April 1962, at which time it was allocated to Exmouth Junction. *Gavin Morrison*

Below: Well cleaned by Salisbury shed, *Croydon* makes a fine sight at the head of an evening express from Waterloo in 1966. *Brian Stephenson*

Above: During its one-year loan to the Great Eastern, when it was allocated to Stratford shed between 12 May 1951 and 17 May 1952, *Biggin Hill* coasts down Brentwood Bank with a Norwich–Liverpool Street express in 1951. *C. R. L. Coles / Rail Archive Stephenson*

Below: Whilst allocated to Brighton *Biggin Hill* passes Cosham on an express for Plymouth in August 1963. *Neville Stead collection*

21C157 *Biggin Hill*

Entered service:	8 March 1947
'Wedge' cab fitted:	November 1947
Renumbered:	34057, 17 June 1949
BR green livery:	April 1951
Mileage (total):	939,597
Withdrawn:	7 May 1967
Fate:	Cut up Cashmores, Newport, October 1967

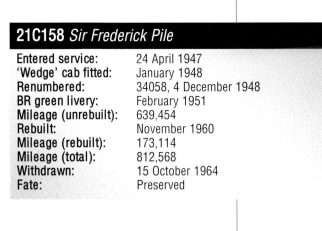

21C158 *Sir Frederick Pile*

Entered service:	24 April 1947
'Wedge' cab fitted:	January 1948
Renumbered:	34058, 4 December 1948
BR green livery:	February 1951
Mileage (unrebuilt):	639,454
Rebuilt:	November 1960
Mileage (rebuilt):	173,114
Mileage (total):	812,568
Withdrawn:	15 October 1964
Fate:	Preserved

Right: Named by Sir Frederick Pile at Waterloo on 28 April 1948, No 34058 heads a slow Plymouth–Exeter train past the atmospheric pumping station at Starcross on 8 September 1955. A few Southern Region trains were diagrammed via this line to maintain crew route knowledge.
R. O. Tuck /
Rail Archive Stephenson

Above: During its brief life of three years 11 months as a rebuilt engine, No 34058 only covered 173,114 miles. This was almost the lowest for any rebuild. Here it is seen on 8 June 1963 leaving Platform 4 at Bournemouth Central, with the shed in the background and Milepost 108¾ from Waterloo in the foreground. Having spent more than 12 years at Exmouth Junction, the locomotive was to spend its final year allocated to Eastleigh.
Gavin Morrison

Left: Only four months old, an unnamed 21C159 makes a fine sight at the head of the down 'Bournemouth Belle' at Waterloo on 16 July 1947. It was named by Sir Archibald Sinclair on 24 February 1948 at Waterloo. *J. P. Wilson / Rail Archive Stephenson*

21C159 *Sir Archibald Sinclair*

Entered service:	3 April 1947
'Wedge' cab fitted:	December 1947
Renumbered:	34059, 11 March 1949
BR green livery:	April 1951
Mileage (unrebuilt):	569,603
Rebuilt:	March 1960
Mileage (rebuilt):	307,504
Mileage (total):	877,107
Withdrawn:	29 May 1966
Fate:	Preserved

Left: During its very brief one-month stay on the Great Eastern, *Sir Archibald Sinclair* storms up the bank near Ingrave Summit with the down 'Norfolkman' on 18 May 1949. The locomotive received a hostile reception from some crews, and no further loans were made for a further 20 months, after which three members of the class were transferred to the Eastern Region. *F. R. Hebron / Rail Archive Stephenson*

Left: During its last 11 years allocated to Salisbury, *Sir Archibald Sinclair* heads an up milk tanker train at 8pm near Milborne Port, between Sherborne and Templecombe, on 18 May 1964. *M. Mensing*

21C160 *25 Squadron*	
Entered service:	25 April 1947
'Wedge' cab fitted:	September 1948
Renumbered:	34060, October 1948
BR green livery:	November 1951
Mileage (unrebuilt):	645,723
Rebuilt:	November 1960
Mileage (rebuilt):	288,694
Mileage (total):	934,417
Withdrawn:	9 June 1967
Fate:	Cut up Cashmores, Newport, September 1968

Above: With the help at the rear from an 'N'-class Mogul, *25 Squadron* climbs the 1 in 36 from Ilfracombe to Mortehoe (near Braunton) with a Waterloo express during September 1960. *Derek Cross*

Right: At the head of an up express to Waterloo, a rather dirty *25 Squadron* is ready to leave Bournemouth West on 29 August 1965. No 34060 was an Eastleigh-allocated engine for the last 2½ years of its life, having spent 12 years previously at Exmouth Junction. *Gavin Morrison*

21C161 *73 Squadron*

Entered service:	25 April 1947
'Wedge' cab fitted:	January 1949
Renumbered:	34061, 21 February 1949
BR green livery:	October 1949
Mileage (total):	701,443
Withdrawn:	18 August 1964
Fate:	Cut up Woods, Queenborough, March 1965

Above: With its BR number and in malachite green, but nothing on the tender, *73 Squadron* has an easy task with this four-coach down local as it leaves Winchfield at mid-day on 15 April 1949. *E. C. Griffith / Rail Archive Stephenson*

Left: 73 Squadron was widely allocated during its career, enjoying spells in Kent, the West Country and at Eastleigh. It is shown on Bournemouth shed on 8 June 1963. *Gavin Morrison*

21C162 *17 Squadron*

Entered service:	30 May 1947
'Wedge' cab fitted:	February 1949
Renumbered:	34062, 17 February 1949
BR green livery:	December 1949
Mileage (unrebuilt):	543,488
Rebuilt:	28 March 1959
Mileage (rebuilt):	293,088
Mileage (total):	836,576
Withdrawn:	8 August 1964
Fate:	Cut up Birds, Bridgend, June 1965 to June 1966

Right: 17 Squadron was transferred to Exmouth Junction on 27 June 1957, where it remained until withdrawn. It is seen piloting No 34024 *Tamar Valley* down the 1 in 37 from Exeter Central to St Davids with a local train for Plymouth or further west on 19 August 1952. *Gavin Morrison*

Right: No 34062 *17 Squadron* is recorded on the ash pits at Nine Elms awaiting attention on 13 September 1958. *Gavin Morrison*

Below right: In dirty condition, *17 Squadron* passes under Battledown Flyover with an up Salisbury–Waterloo train on 19 September 1961. In rebuilt form, the locomotive averaged 55,826 miles per annum, the third-highest average for a rebuild. *D. M. C. Hepburne-Scott / Rail Archive Stephenson*

Below: The nameplate and crest as mounted on the rebuilt locomotives. No 34062 *17 Squadron*. *J. F. Davies / Rail Archive Stephenson*

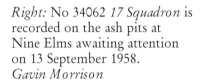

Left: Prior to being named, No 21C163 reverses out of Victoria with the empty stock off a Margate train on 4 March 1948. At this date the locomotive was only 10 months old and allocated to Ramsgate. *E. Bruton / Pendragon Collection*

21C163 *229 Squadron*

Entered service:	29 May 1947
'Wedge' cab fitted:	January 1949
Renumbered:	34063, June 1949
BR green livery:	July 1951
Mileage (total):	736,984
Withdrawn:	15 August 1965
Fate:	Cut up Birds, Bridgend, May 1966

Below: 229 Squadron crosses the River Taw as it sets off from Barnstaple Town with the 2.20pm Ilfracombe–Waterloo service on 19 May 1959. *K. L. Cook / Rail Archive Stephenson*

21C164 *Fighter Command*

Entered service:	14 July 1947
Renumbered:	34064, 3 June 1948
BR green livery:	June 1950
Mileage (total):	759,666
Withdrawn:	22 May 1966
Fate:	Cut up Birds, Bridgend, November 1966
Notes:	1,000th locomotive to be built at Brighton Works

Right: This is an official picture of No 21C164 as it emerged from Brighton Works. No 21C164 was the first to be fitted with a new 'wedge' cab front plate and angled windows, although retaining the two cabside windows. It was claimed this modification increased visibility ahead by over 30%. *Ian Allan Library*

Left: Fighter Command was named at Waterloo on 11 September 1947 by Sir James Robb. It was one of the seven members of the class to run in the experimental apple-green livery with cream bands edged with red and grey, operating in this condition between 11 June 1948 and 24 June 1950. During its last general overhaul in April 1962 it was fitted with a Giesl ejector and spark arrester, although no official trials were done. It would appear that this modification did not do anything for the locomotive's performance and, it has been said, it made the locomotive more difficult to fire. Here it is seen passing Clapham Junction with the 11.30am Waterloo-Bournemouth service on 30 May 1964 with the Giesl ejector clearly visible. *Brian Stephenson*

Left: Fighter Command on shed at Eastleigh on 12 September 1964. This was the only member of the class to receive the Giesl ejector. *Gavin Morrison*

21C165 *Hurricane*

Entered service:	8 July 1947
Renumbered:	34065, 12 June 1948
BR green livery:	July 1951
Mileage (total):	730,489
Withdrawn:	April 1964
Fate:	Cut up Birds, Swansea, November 1964

Above: A fine rear view of the No 21C165, seen when nearly new, illustrates the impressive malachite-green livery and lining. The locomotive ran in apple-green livery between 12 June 1948 and 14 March 1951.
Pendragon Collection

Right: A pleasant study of *Hurricane* calling at Axminster with a down train on 16 August 1960, at which time it was allocated to Exmouth Junction. It was named at Waterloo on 16 September 1947 by Sir Frank Spriggs.
A. Tyson / Pendragon Collection

21C166 *Spitfire*

Entered service:	5 September 1947
Renumbered:	34066, 19 February 1949
BR green livery:	May 1950
Mileage (total):	652,908
Withdrawn:	10 September 1966
Fate:	Cut up at Buttigiegs, Newport, January 1967

Right: The name *Spitfire* ensured that No 34066 was one of the best-known members of the class, but it was the serious accident at St Johns on 4 December 1957 for which it will always be remembered. Ninety people died, and a further 108 were seriously injured. The locomotive ran into the back of an electric unit at 30mph in the fog whilst working the 4.56pm Cannon Street–Dover express. Unfortunately the collision occurred under the flyover, causing the girders to collapse onto the train. The failure of the flyover was the reason for the majority of the deaths and injuries, not the original impact. *Spitfire* was only out of traffic for around a month. Under happier circumstances, it is seen pulling away from Pokesdown station with a down Bournemouth train on 23 July 1966.
Gavin Morrison

Right: After stopping at Pokesdown, *Spitfire* is seen climbing the bank to Branksome with assistance in the rear with a Summer Saturdays Poole–Newcastle express on 29 July 1966. *Gavin Morrison*

Left: In service for 16 years and two months, *Tangmere* spent 12 years allocated to Stewarts Lane. On 18 May 1949, during its years at this London shed, the locomotive is seen on the turntable at its home depot with the 's' prefix in front of its original number and with 'BRITISH RAILWAYS' on the tender. *Tangmere* was one of 22 locomotives to receive the 's' prefix. *J. P. Wilson / Rail Archive Stephenson*

21C167 *Tangmere*

Entered service:	3 September 1947
Renumbered:	34067, 20 July 1949
BR green livery:	April 1951
Mileage (total):	688,269
Withdrawn:	16 November 1963
Fate:	Preserved

Left: Tangmere is recorded heading a down Kent Coast express away from Faversham past the locomotive shed, which contains a good selection of ex-South Eastern & Chatham locomotives, on 10 July 1952. *P. Lynch*

Right: Tangmere was named at Brighton on 19 September 1947 by Wing-Commander Clouston. During the period of two-and-a-half years it was allocated to Salisbury before withdrawal, it is seen on shed complete with the appropriate squadron badge on the cabside on 23 April 1962. Today No 34067 is regularly seen out on the main line, particularly in the south of England. *Gavin Morrison*

Below: Kenley was allocated to Stewarts Lane for 11½ years, but it ended its days at Salisbury. Withdrawn three weeks earlier, it is seen here having arrived at Eastleigh shed. The locomotive presents a sorry sight on 28 December 1963 prior to making its last journey to the works for cutting up. *Gavin Morrison*

21C168 *Kenley*

Entered service:	7 October 1947
Renumbered:	34068, 30 September 1948
BR green livery:	September 1950
Mileage (total):	700,417
Withdrawn:	7 December 1963
Fate:	Cut up Eastleigh Works 21 March 1964

21C169 *Hawkinge*

Entered service:	29 October 1947
Renumbered:	34069, 30 September 1948
BR green livery:	October 1952
Mileage (total):	673,643
Withdrawn:	23 November 1963
Fate:	Cut up Eastleigh Works 16 May 1964

Right: Hawkinge spent virtually its entire career at Stewarts Lane and Exmouth Junction. It was one of the nine withdrawn in 1963, the first year of withdrawals for the class. Here it is pictured heading a down relief to the 'Atlantic Coast Express' past Brookwood in September 1960. *Derek Cross*

21C170 Manston

Entered service:	21 October 1947
Renumbered:	34070, 31 March 1949
BR green livery:	March 1953
Mileage (total):	702,614
Withdrawn:	5 September 1964
Fate:	Preserved

Right: Being a Ramsgate-allocated locomotive *Manston* was selected for the inaugural run of the 'Thanet Belle' summer only Pullman service from Victoria to Ramsgate on 31 May 1948. The train's last titled run was on 24 September 1950. *Pendragon Collection*

Right: Still running as 21C170, with the Southern roundel on the smokebox and in malachite-green livery but with 'BRITISH RAILWAYS' on the tender, *Manston* makes a fine sight heading the 12.45pm from Cannon Street soon after Nationalisation. It was the last of the class to enter service with the Bulleid numbers as well as being the last of the class to retain malachite-green livery.
R. A. Reaves

34071 601 Squadron

Entered service:	17 April 1948
BR green livery:	February 1952
Mileage (unrebuilt):	437,599
Rebuilt:	May 1960
Mileage (rebuilt):	344,429
Mileage (total):	782,028
Withdrawn:	30 April 1967
Fate:	Cut up Cashmores, Newport, September 1967

Right: 601 Squadron was named at Brighton on 15 September 1948 by Group Captain Max Aitken. It is shown heading for Dover or Folkestone with a boat train near Hildenbrough, between Sevenoaks and Tonbridge, on 23 May 1953.
Brian Morrison

Left: At the head of an express to Waterloo, *601 Squadron* passes through Hinton Admiral in the New Forest on 18 August 1961. *Gavin Morrison*

Below: The 1.30pm Victoria–Folkestone 'Continental Express' passes Tonbridge with *257 Squadron* acting as pilot to 'L1' class 4-4-0 No 31753 on 2 October 1954. *Ian Allan Library*

34072 *257 Squadron*

Entered service:	24 April 1948
BR green livery:	April 1952
Mileage (total):	698,843
Withdrawn:	25 October 1964
Fate:	preserved

Above: A fine portrait of *257 Squadron* when probably less than a year old on Stewarts Lane complete with 'Night Ferry' headboard. It was the first of the class to be built with the 9ft-wide 'wedge' cab; the previously fitted 'wedge' cabs had been 8ft 6in wide. *Rail Archive Stephenson*

Left: After spending its first 10 years in service allocated to Dover, *257 Squadron* moved to Exmouth Junction for six-and-a-half years, during which period it was photographed shunting empty stock to form the 10.30am to Waterloo from Ilfracombe — the 'Atlantic Coast Express' — on 18 May 1959. *K. L. Cook / Rail Archive Stephenson*

Left: 249 Squadron approaches Faversham with an up express from Margate in the early 1950s. The steam shed can just be seen in the background. *Ian Allan Library*

34073 *249 Squadron*	
Entered service:	6 May 1948
BR green livery:	December 1950
Mileage (total):	684,325
Withdrawn:	28 June 1964
Fate:	Preserved

Left: No 34073 went new to Ramsgate for seven months then spent over 12 years at Dover before moving to Nine Elms, where it is seen on the shed on 14 October 1962. *Gavin Morrison*

34074 *46 Squadron*

Entered service:	27 May 1948
BR green livery:	September 1952
Mileage (total):	639,592
Withdrawn:	15 June 1963
Fate:	Cut up Eastleigh Works 30 May 1964

Right: Before being named, No 34074, with front numberplate and painted BR number, leaves Victoria with the 3pm boat train on 4 July 1949. It was later to be one of the first members of the class withdrawn. *J. P. Wilson / Rail Archive Stephenson*

34075 *264 Squadron*

Entered service:	9 June 1948
BR green livery:	September 1952
Mileage (total):	643,241
Withdrawn:	April 1964
Fate:	Cut up Birds, Bridgend, June 1965 to June 1966

Above: Taken prior to being named and with its BR number painted in the original position, No 34075 blows off as it shuts off heading a South Eastern Division express. The date is probably around early 1949. *Ian Allan Library*

Right: An unusual viewpoint of *41 Squadron* as it heads an up Dover-London express through Folkestone on 31 July 1955. *J. F. Davies / Rail Archive Stephenson*

34076 *41 Squadron*

Entered service:	26 June 1948
BR green livery:	September 1950
Mileage (total):	803,425
Withdrawn:	9 January 1966
Fate:	Cut up Cashmores, Newport, November 1966

34077 *603 Squadron*

Entered service:	10 July 1948
BR green livery:	August 1951
Mileage (unrebuilt):	478,162
Rebuilt:	July 1960
Mileage (rebuilt):	267,480
Mileage (total):	745,642
Withdrawn:	26 March 1967
Fate:	Cut up Cashmores, Newport, August 1967

Above: 603 Squadron was a South Eastern Division locomotive for nearly 13 years before moving to Nine Elms. Here it is seen on 26 February 1960 heading a down express near Tudeley, east of Tonbridge, during the period when it was allocated to Stewarts Lane (73A). *D. M. C. Hepburne-Scott / Rail Archive Stephenson*

Left: A 'Continental Express' leaves a siding at Folkestone Junction for Victoria behind *603 Squadron* on 1 March 1961. The train had been hauled up the steep incline from the harbour by two ex-Great Western 0-6-0PTs. *M. Edwards*

34078 *222 Squadron*

Entered service:	21 July 1948
BR green livery:	August 1951
Mileage (total):	779,643
Withdrawn:	September 1964
Fate:	Cut up Birds, Morriston, Swansea, December 1964

Below: Still looking smart in its malachite-green livery but with 'British Railways' on the tender, No 34078 *222 Squadron* heads a down express from London Bridge through the South London suburbs on 5 April 1951. It was one of the few members of the class to keep its original 5,500gal tender, complete with raves, until the end. *Brian Morrison*

34079 *141 Squadron*

Entered service:	23 July 1948
BR green livery:	May 1951
Mileage (total):	765,302
Withdrawn:	27 February 1966
Fate:	Cut up Cashmores, Newport, 1966

Right: Three members of the class received the lion-and-wheel BR emblem whilst still retaining the malachite-green livery. No 34079 *141 Squadron* is seen in this condition; the other two were Nos 34036 and 34071. This photograph was taken at Tonbridge *c*1949. *C. R. L. Coles / Rail Archive Stephenson*

Right: A fine study of *141 Squadron* at Cannon Street as the locomotive is ready to leave with a Ramsgate train on 23 July 1955. From new No 34079 spent just over 10 years at Ramsgate before being reallocated to Exmouth Junction. In the background can be seen pioneer 'Schools' class 4-4-0 No 30900 *Eton*. *J. F. Davies / Rail Archive Stephenson*

34080 *74 Squadron*

Entered service:	20 August 1948
BR green livery:	August 1951
Mileage (total):	749,863
Withdrawn:	September 1964
Fate:	Cut up Birds, Morriston, Swansea, December 1964

Below: 74 Squadron, allocated to Ramsgate, makes an impressive departure from Victoria with a down express for the Kent Coast in the mid-1950s. *D. Callms*

34081 *92 Squadron*

Entered service:	10 September 1948
BR green livery:	April 1950
Mileage (total):	741,511
Withdrawn:	16 August 1964
Fate:	Preserved

Below: 92 Squadron was new to Ramsgate, where it spent nine years before moving to Exmouth Junction. This undated picture, taken during its allocation to Ramsgate, shows it departing Dover Western Docks with an up express. *Neville Stead collection*

Right: 92 Squadron makes a fine sight at the head of the up 'Man of Kent' as it passes Shorncliffe in this undated view. The inaugural run of the train was on 8 June 1953 and the last titled run was on 10 June 1961. The service ran from Charing Cross to Margate.
T. G. Hepburn / Rail Archive Stephenson

34082 *615 Squadron*

Entered service	24 September 1948
BR green livery:	September 1950
Mileage (unrebuilt):	424,406
Rebuilt:	April 1960
Mileage (rebuilt):	272,980
Mileage (total):	697,386
Withdrawn:	24 April 1966
Fate:	Cut up Cashmores, Newport, September 1966

Right: 615 Squadron was allocated to Dover between 10 April 1958 and 26 May 1961, when it moved to Nine Elms. It is seen here in May 1959 on the prestigious up 'Golden Arrow' passing Paddock Wood. It was the last 'Battle of Britain' to have an official naming ceremony, which was performed by Sir Malcolm Fraser at Guildford on 8 October 1948. It was also the first of the class to be fitted with a smokebox numberplate from new although also provided with a number on the front buffer-beam. *B. Coates*

Right: 615 Squadron climbs the bank out of Brockenhurst across the common with a Waterloo–Bournemouth West express on 9 September 1965. *Gavin Morrison*

34083 *605 Squadron*

Entered service:	14 October 1948
BR green livery:	September 1952
Mileage (total):	737,464
Withdrawn:	8 August 1964
Fate:	Cut up Birds, Bridgend, June 1965 to June 1966

Below: Taken in the spring of 1949 before the locomotive was named, this is an impressive portrait of No 34083 on the turntable at Dover Marine when on 'Golden Arrow' duties. It went new to Stewarts Lane shed and stayed there until 12 May 1951 when it was reallocated to Ramsgate. *A. W. Croughton / Rail Archive Stephenson*

34084 *253 Squadron*

Entered service:	4 November 1948
BR green livery:	March 1950
Mileage (total):	663,249
Withdrawn:	3 October 1965
Fate:	Cut up Buttigiegs, Newport, March 1966

Above: Wintry conditions in Kent see *253 Squadron* heading the down 'Golden Arrow' across the Kentish Weald on 11 January 1960. *Derek Cross*

Right: The impressive station clock rises above *253 Squadron* as it prepares to leave Southampton Central at 12.7pm with a Summer Saturday cross-country service on 12 September 1966. *Gavin Morrison*

34085 *501 Squadron*

Entered service:	19 November 1948
BR green livery:	March 1950
Mileage (unrebuilt):	441,609
Rebuilt:	June 1960
Mileage (rebuilt):	219,806
Mileage (total):	661,415
Withdrawn:	26 September 1965
Fate:	Cut up Buttigiegs, Newport, April 1966

Above: 501 Squadron was a regular performer on the 'Golden Arrow' and other Continental expresses during its two and a half years at Stewarts Lane where it went when new. On 9 December 1949 it was involved in an accident when working light engine, colliding with the incoming 'Golden Arrow' at slow speed outside Victoria. Here it is heading the down train past Factory Junction in South London; note the ordinary stock at the front of the train. This was the last 'Battle of Britain' to be named, on 30 July 1955. *R. C. Riley / Transport Treasury*

Left: 501 Squadron is seen at the head of the northbound 'Pines Express' near Hinton Admiral on 7 August 1965. The consist includes both ex-LMS carriages and one LNER coach (second vehicle in the rake). No 34085 was allocated to Bournemouth from 17 January 1961 until withdrawal. *D. M. C. Hepburne-Scott / Rail Archive Stephenson*

34086 *219 Squadron*

Entered service:	2 December 1948
BR green livery:	October 1950
Mileage (total):	700,982
Withdrawn:	25 June 1966
Fate:	Cut up Buttigiegs, Newport, November 1966

Above: 219 Squadron is seen alongside BR '9F' No 92052, which had arrived at Clapham Junction with an 18-coach empty-stock working, on 12 August 1960. The stock was going to be taken forward to Lewes via Tulse Hill by *219 Squadron* and 'U1' class 2-6-0 No 31895, which can just be seen. Ivatt 2-6-2T No 41292 was on shunting duties. No 34086 ran in the experimental apple-green livery between 2 December 1948 and 11 October 1950. *J. Scrace*

Right: One month before being transferred away from Exmouth Junction to Eastleigh *219 Squadron*, looking well cleaned, is seen coasting towards Wilton station, which closed on 7 March 1966, heading the 11.30am Brighton–Plymouth service on 3 August 1964. *M. Mensing*

34087 *145 Squadron*

Entered service:	17 December 1948
BR green livory:	October 1950
Mileage (unrebuilt):	415,738
Rebuilt:	December 1960
Mileage (rebuilt):	288,900
Mileage (total):	704,638
Withdrawn:	9 September 1967
Fate:	Cut up Cashmores, Newport, April to September 1968

Left: 145 Squadron passes Selling on a Victoria–Dover Marine express diverted via Chatham on 12 January 1958. The locomotive ran in the experimental apple-green livery between 17 December 1948 and 25 October 1950. *J. Head*

Above: 145 Squadron, running with a 9ft wide 5,500gal tender complete with a shrouded lamp in the centre to assist coupling at night, leaves Bournemouth West on 22 April 1962 for Central where it will combine with a portion from Weymouth before heading for Waterloo. *145 Squadron* will then head for the shed for servicing. *Gavin Morrison*

34088 213 Squadron

Entered service:	22 December 1948
BR green livery:	December 1950
Mileage (unrebuilt):	377,016
Rebuilt:	April 1960
Mileage (rebuilt):	279,567
Mileage (total):	656,583
Withdrawn:	March 1967
Fate:	Cut up Cashmores, Newport, March 1968

Left: 213 Squadron was the last of the seven members of the class to receive the experimental apple-green livery, which it carried between 22 December 1948 and 16 December 1950. During its 11 years and four months as an unrebuilt member of the class, it had a low annual mileage average of 33,266. This is possibly due to it spending virtually all its time prior to rebuilding on the South Eastern Division; low annual mileages were also recorded for Nos 34087 and 34089, both of which spent similar periods on the South Eastern. This fine picture taken in the 1950s shows *213 Squadron* leaving Folkestone with some help in the rear, probably from the locomotives which had brought the train up the bank from Folkestone Harbour.
Pendragon Collection

Right As with the 'Merchant Navies', in spite of all the experiments and front-end modifications to the class, the problem of drifting smoke causing a big safety problem for the crew was never really solved on the unrebuilt locomotives. This dramatic picture of *213 Squadron* illustrates the problem perfectly as it heads the 9.30am Victoria–Ramsgate express near Swanley on 8 November 1952.
Brian Morrison

Right: This is a fine study of *213 Squadron* leaving Tunbridge Wells West with an empty-stock movement to New Cross Gate on 16 June 1963.
Ian Allan Library

34089 *602 Squadron*

Entered service:	December 1948
BR green livery:	June 1950
Mileage (unrebuilt):	402,834
Rebuilt:	November 1960
Mileage (rebuilt):	258,418
Mileage (total):	661,252
Withdrawn:	9 July 1967
Fate:	Cut up Cashmores, Newport, April to September 1968

Left: On a dull day, an immaculate *602 Squadron* leaves Victoria with the down 'Golden Arrow' in 1960. Unrebuilt, it averaged 33,804 miles per annum over almost 12 years; following rebuilding it managed to average an annual mileage of 38,763 in six years eight months. *Pendragon Collection*

Left: The white cliffs show up well looking towards Dover in this picture of *602 Squadron* heading the up 'Golden Arrow' past Folkestone Warren in June 1960. *Derek Cross*

Below: Now minus its nameplate, No 34089 reverses off Bournemouth shed to work an up express to Waterloo on 27 March 1967. *Gavin Morrison*

Right: Sir Eustace Missenden, Southern Railway didn't make it into service until February 1949 so was a BR engine. The PR department of Southern Region decided it should receive the name of the Southern Railway's last general manager at a ceremony on 15 February 1949 at Waterloo. The locomotive was painted in malachite green, including the wheels which would normally have been black, plus additional yellow lining, all of which must have presented quite a sight. The BR lion-and-wheel emblem was on the tender. Here No 34090, when allocated to Nine Elms, is seen in the more sombre BR Brunswick green heading a down express for Weymouth past Weybridge in May 1959. *Derek Cross*

34090 *Sir Eustace Missenden, Southern Railway*

Entered service:	1 February 1949
BR green livery:	March 1952
Mileage (unrebuilt):	444,006
Rebuilt:	August 1960
Mileage (rebuilt):	299,937
Mileage (total):	743,943
Withdrawn:	9 July 1967
Fate:	Cut up Cashmores, Newport, March 1968

Above: By now allocated to Salisbury and showing its impressive large nameplate, *Sir Eustace Missenden, Southern Railway*, in fine external condition, departs from Waterloo with the 11.30am service to Bournemouth on 8 March 1964. This was the last locomotive in what was expected to be the final batch of Bulleid Pacifics; however, this did not prove to be the case. *G. D. King*

34091 Weymouth

Entered service:	September 1949
BR green livery:	From new
Mileage (total):	469,073
Withdrawn:	September 1964
Fate:	Cut up Woods, Queenborough, December 1964 to March 1965

Left: Weymouth was only allocated to two sheds during its career: its first 11½ years saw the locomotive based at Stewarts Lane and the rest of its life was spent at Salisbury. Along with *City of Wells* it was frequently diagrammed for the 'Golden Arrow'. It is seen being prepared at Folkestone Junction, complete with full embellishments, on 2 October 1955 for duty on the 'Golden Arrow'. It was the last 'West Country' to be named formally, by the then mayor of Weymouth (Alderman A. P. Burt), on 29 December 1949. It had a very low average mileage of 31,272 per annum, the second lowest for an unrebuilt engine. *J. F. Davies / Rail Archive Stephenson*

Left: This may well have been amongst the last workings for *Weymouth*, as it was withdrawn in September 1964. In rather dirty condition, it is pictured ready to leave Eastleigh station with an evening train for Portsmouth, probably a cross-country working, on 12 September 1964. *Gavin Morrison*

34092 City of Wells

Entered service:	September 1949
BR green livery:	From new
Mileage (total):	502,864
Withdrawn:	29 November 1964
Fate:	Preserved
Note:	Originally named *Wells* until March *1950*

Below: City of Wells was unusual for a member of the class because it was only allocated to two sheds during its career. Almost 12 years were spent at Stewarts Lane and the rest at Salisbury. It was a regular performer on the 'Golden Arrow' and is seen in this picture at Knockholt with the down express in September 1959. Its mileage average was low at 33,156 per annum, no doubt due to the length of time spent at Stewarts Lane. Based at the Keighley & Worth Valley Railway, it was a regular performer on the main line in preservation; it has been undergoing a major rebuild for several years. *Derek Cross*

34093 *Saunton*

Entered service:	October 1949
BR green livery:	From new
Mileage (unrebuilt):	528,389
Rebuilt:	May 1960
Mileage (rebuilt):	359,615
Mileage (total):	888,004
Withdrawn:	9 July 1967
Fate:	Cut up Cashmores, Newport, March 1968

Right: No 34093 spent almost 10 years at Bournemouth before moving to Nine Elms on 6 June 1958. It is seen here on Nine Elms shed after working the 'Royal Wessex' on 21 August 1954. *Brian Morrison*

Above: On 11 September 1960, only four months after being rebuilt and reallocated to Nine Elms, *Saunton* is pictured on Eastleigh shed. *Gavin Morrison*

Right: Now allocated to Eastleigh, *Saunton* passes Totton with an up express from Bournemouth to Waterloo on 9 September 1965. *Gavin Morrison*

34094 *Mortehoe*

Entered service:	October 1949
BR green livery:	From new
Mileage (total):	672,346
Withdrawn:	August 1964
Fate:	Cut up Woodham Bros, Barry, November 1964

Above: Mortehoe is shown just to the east of Basingstoke, heading the 11am Bournemouth West–Waterloo on 4 August 1958. *M. Mensing*

Below: Withdrawn the previous month, *Mortehoe* looks respectably clean at Eastleigh on 12 September 1964 as it awaits its final journey to South Wales. Behind is a BR Class 9F 2-10-0. *Gavin Morrison*

34095 *Brentor*

Entered service:	October 1949
BR green livery:	From new
Mileage (unrebuilt):	566,629
Rebuilt:	January 1961
Mileage (rebuilt):	229,985
Mileage (total):	796,614
Withdrawn:	9 July 1967
Fate:	Cut up Cashmores, Newport, April 1968

Right: *Brentor* was built at Eastleigh Works and went new to Bournemouth, where it stayed until January 1956. During its time at Bournemouth it is shown on 25 June 1951 heading the down 'Royal Wessex' near Clapham Junction overtaking '2-BIL' electric unit No 2142. The 'Royal Wessex' was an express from Weymouth/Swanage/Bournemouth West to Waterloo (the three portions combining *en route*), leaving Weymouth at around 7.30am and returning at 4.35pm. This service ran from 3 May 1951 to 8 July 1967.
Gavin Morrison

Right: Framed by the superb signal gantry at the west end of Southampton Central, *Brentor* prepares to leave with a down express on 12 September 1964.
Gavin Morrison

Left: *Brentor* pulls away from Christchurch station on a hot summer's day with a down express as it heads onto the 1 in 99 climb to Pokesdown on 9 June 1962.
Gavin Morrison

34096 *Trevone*

Entered service:	November 1949
BR green livery:	From new
Mileage (unrebuilt):	511,280
Rebuilt:	April 1961
Mileage (rebuilt):	211,046
Mileage (total):	722,326
Withdrawn:	September 1964
Fate:	Cut up Birds, Bynea, March 1965

Left: Trevone, in poor external condition and allocated to Exmouth Junction, pulls out of Wadebridge with the up 'Atlantic Coast Express' — all two coaches of it — on 8 July 1960. During its career No 34096 was only allocated to Ramsgate and Exmouth Junction sheds. *J. C. Haydon*

Above: Another easy duty for *Trevone* as it heads the 5pm Waterloo–Yeovil Town working out of Milborne Port Halt on 18 May 1964. Following rebuilding, No 34096 only had three years five months of service, but managed to achieve the highest annual mileage for a rebuilt member of the class with 61,770 miles per annum. *M. Mensing*

34097 Holsworthy

Entered service:	November 1949
BR green livery:	From new
Mileage (unrebuilt):	500,111
Rebuilt:	March 1961
Mileage (rebuilt):	243,548
Mileage (total):	743,659
Withdrawn:	April 1966
Fate:	Cut up Cashmores,

Left: Eastleigh-built *Holsworthy*, pictured whilst allocated to Brighton, is seen at the head of the 6.10pm service from Victoria near South Croydon during August 1960. *R. Russell*

Below: Seen just to the east of Bournemouth Central station on 10 September 1965, *Holsworthy* heads an up Waterloo express. An Eastleigh-built engine, No 34097 was by this date allocated to Eastleigh shed and is recorded in terrible external condition.
Gavin Morrison

34098 Templecombe

Entered service:	December 1949
BR green livery:	From new
Mileage (unrebuilt):	535,630
Rebuilt:	February 1961
Mileage (rebuilt):	283,475
Mileage (total):	819,105
Withdrawn:	June 1967
Fate:	Cut up Buttigiegs, Newport, November 1967

Right: Templecombe was allocated to Brighton between 11 March 1959 and 24 November 1960, during which time the locomotive is leaving Brighton with a train to Bournemouth. *J. Davenport*

Right: Templecombe pulls away from Branksome with some empty stock to form a working from Bournemouth Central on 26 December 1966. It would appear that Eastleigh shed had no cleaners available at this time.
Gavin Morrison

34099 Lynmouth

Entered service:	December 1949
BR green livery:	From new
Mileage (total):	628,771
Withdrawn:	November 1964
Fate:	Cut up Birds, Morriston, Swansea, March 1965

Left: Eastleigh-built *Lynmouth* is heading the 'Man of Kent', which ran between Charing Cross and Margate between 8 June 1953 and 10 June 1961, and is seen here passing Hildenborough on 22 April 1957, when allocated to Ramsgate. *K. L. Cook / Rail Archive Stephenson*

34100 *Appledore*

Entered service:	December 1949
BR green livery:	From new
Mileage (unrebuilt):	409,318
Rebuilt:	September 1960
Mileage (rebuilt):	303,598
Mileage (total):	712,916
Withdrawn:	9 July 1967
Fate:	Cut up Cashmores, Newport, October 1967

Right: Another of the Eastleigh-built locomotives seen under the impressive overall roof at Cannon Street station, *Appledore* is ready to depart with a down express on 25 April 1952. *Brian Morrison*

Above: Still in fine condition six months after rebuilding, *Appledore* passes Chart siding, near Ashford, with the down 'Golden Arrow' Pullman on 4 March 1961. The locomotive was allocated to Stewarts Lane at the time. *J. Head / Rail Archive Stephenson*

Right: In marked contrast to the external condition in the previous picture, *Appledore* is seen at Bournemouth West carriage sidings with some empty stock on 18 April 1965. *Gavin Morrison*

34101 *Hartland*

Entered service:	February 1950
BR green livery:	From new
Mileage (unrebuilt):	330,106
Rebuilt:	September 1960
Mileage (rebuilt):	238,373
Mileage (total):	568,479
Withdrawn:	July 1966
Fate:	Preserved

Above: Hartland was a Stewarts Lane engine during the 10 years eight months it ran in unrebuilt condition. This Eastleigh-built locomotive only covered 330,106 miles during this period, giving it the lowest annual mileage for any unrebuilt member of the class. Here it is seen against the White Cliffs, passing the little signalbox at Abbot, about halfway between Folkestone and Dover on the long 12-mile descent from Sandling. *Derek Cross*

Above right: From May 1961, *Hartland* was allocated to Bricklayers Arms for 14 months. During this period, it is seen leaving Eridge with the 1.55pm Brighton–Victoria service on 18 September 1961. *D. Ovenden*

Right: Hartland passes through Bournemouth Central in June 1965 with coal wagons from the yard at the east end probably destined for the shed. It shows tender No 3366, a 9ft wide 5,500gal type. *Derek Cross*

34102 *Lapford*

Entered service:	March 1950
BR green livery:	From new
Mileage (total):	593,438
Withdrawn:	9 July 1967
Fate:	Cut up Buttigiegs, Newport, April to September 1968

Left: Eastleigh-built No 34102 is in fine external condition, *Lapford* passes through Clapham Cutting with the 5.54pm Waterloo–Basingstoke service on 27 June 1964. *Brian Stephenson*

Above: Now minus its nameplate, *Lapford* is seen under repair at Bournemouth shed on 27 March 196/. This would be one of the last two 'West Countries' to be withdrawn (the other being No 34023 *Blackmore Vale*) and during its career of just over 17 years averaged just 34,237 miles per annum. *Gavin Morrison*

34103 *Calstock*

Entered service:	February 1950
BR green livery:	From new
Mileage (total):	629,172
Withdrawn:	September 1965
Fate:	Cut up Buttigiegs, Newport, April 1966

Above: Calstock heads over the famous Battledown Flyover at the head of a boat train from Southampton Docks to Waterloo in May 1960. *Derek Cross*

Right: On 5 March 1950, when less than one month old, *Calstock* is seen on Bournemouth shed, probably being run in by Eastleigh before being sent to Stewarts Lane shed where it was allocated from new for almost seven years. *G. O. P. Pearce*

Right: During the period of almost four years the locomotive was allocated to Bournemouth, *Calstock* is seen heading a down Waterloo–Bournemouth express through the New Forest near Hinton Admiral on 19 August 1961. *Gavin Morrison*

Right: Bere Alston was both the last locomotive to be built at Eastleigh Works and the last of its class to be rebuilt there. Its first eight years were spent on the South Eastern Division before almost three years allocated to Exmouth Junction. During this latter period, it is shown climbing the almost four miles of 1 in 36 out of Ilfracombe with the down 'Atlantic Coast Express' without the help of a banking locomotive. The photograph was taken near Mortehoe in September 1959. *Derek Cross*

34104 *Bere Alston*

Entered service:	April 1950
BR green livery:	From new
Mileage (unrebuilt):	425,977
Rebuilt:	May 1961
Mileage (rebuilt):	252,876
Mileage (total):	678,853
Withdrawn:	June 1967
Fate:	Cut up Buttigiegs, Newport, October 1967 to October 1968

Above: Headed by a very dirty *Bere Alston*, the 9am Waterloo–Plymouth Friary service crosses the River Tavy near the end of its journey on 4 August 1960. *Hugh Ballantyne*

Right: On 10 September 1965 a down Channel Island boat train passes Bournemouth Central Goods (just east of the station) behind *Bere Alston*, attached to unmodified tender No 3313. In the background (right) can be seen 'Merchant Navy' No 35003 *Royal Mail* shunting the coal yard. *Gavin Morrison*

34105 *Swanage*

Entered service:	March 1950
BR green livery:	From new
Mileage (total):	623,405
Withdrawn:	4 October 1964
Fate:	Preserved

Right: Swanage is pictured about to depart Southampton Central with a cross-country service from Bournemouth on 12 September 1964. *Gavin Morrison*

34106 *Lydford*

Entered service:	March 1950
BR green livery:	From new
Mileage (total):	691,443
Withdrawn:	September 1964
Fate:	Cut up Birds, Morriston, Swansea, December 1964

Below: Lydford passes non-stop through Christchurch and onto the 1-in-99 gradient to Pokesdown at the head of a down Waterloo–Bournemouth express on 8 April 1955. *D. M. C. Hepburne-Scott / Rail Archive Stephenson*

34107 *Blandford Forum*	
Entered service:	April 1950
BR green livery:	From new
Mileage (total):	665,130
Withdrawn:	September 1964
Fate:	Cut up Birds, Morriston, Swansea, December 1964
Note:	Named *Blandford* until October 1952

Above: Blandford Forum approaches Eastleigh station on the 19-mile climb from St Denys to Litchfield Tunnel at the head of an up 'Union Castle' boat express from Southampton Docks to Waterloo on 2 July 1954. *Brian Morrison*

Below: Showing the nameplate and crest off well, *Blandford Forum* is on Eastleigh shed awaiting a visit to the works for the last time on 12 April 1963. *Gavin Morrison*

34108 *Wincanton*

Entered service:	April 1950
BR green livery:	From new
Mileage (unrebuilt):	583,780
Rebuilt:	April 1961
Mileage (rebuilt):	224,581
Mileage (total):	808,361
Withdrawn:	June 1967
Fate:	Cut up Buttigiegs, Newport, October 1967 to October 1968

Right: Wincanton spent 11 years in service as an unrebuilt locomotive, during which period it was allocated to Bournemouth, Exmouth Junction and Salisbury sheds. It is seen on the LSWR's four-track main-line at the head of an eight-coach express. *Ian Allan Library*

Right: The driver has a chat with a colleague whilst very dirty rebuilt *Wincanton* waits to leave Bournemouth West with the up 'Bournemouth Belle' on 29 July 1962. A dual-carriageway road now runs through this location. *Gavin Morrison*

Right: Just about at the summit of the difficult 1 in 90/101 climb out of Bournemouth West to the junction, *Wincanton* is about to take the east side of the triangle to Gas Works Junction with the up 'Bournemouth Belle' on 29 July 1962. *Gavin Morrison*

34109 *Sir Trafford Leigh Mallory*

Entered service:	May 1950
BR green livery:	From new
Mileage (unrebuilt):	557,217
Rebuilt:	March 1961
Mileage (rebuilt):	162,601
Mileage (total):	719,818
Withdrawn:	September 1964
Fate:	Cut up Birds, Morriston, Swansea, December 1964

Left: The 'Bournemouth Belle' is seen at its best with immaculate *Sir Trafford Leigh Mallory* heading the down train near Hinton Admiral on 31 May 1954. The train carried three different types of headboard during its career; this was the third type, which was introduced in the summer of 1953. The train ran between July 1931 and 9 July 1967 except during World War 2.
D. M. C. Hepburne-Scott / Rail Archive Stephenson

Above: In rebuilt form *Sir Trafford Leigh Mallory* only lasted three-and-a-half years and covered 162,601 miles, statistics which hardly justified the expense of rebuilding. It is seen on Bournemouth shed when allocated to Exmouth Junction surrounded by other members of the class, Nos 34085, 34108, 34059 and 34040, on 13 September 1964, the month during which it was withdrawn. *Gavin Morrison*

34110 *66 Squdron*

Entered service:	26 January 1951
BR green livery:	From new
Mileage (total):	609,147
Withdrawn:	22 November 1963
Fate:	Cut up Eastleigh Works 28 March 1964

Above: There was a seven-month gap between Nos 34109 and 34110 entering service, leading perhaps to the rumour that it was to be built without Bulleid's valve gear; this, however, did not prove to be the case. It was the final member of the class to be constructed, becoming a 'Battle of Britain' although not appearing to receive the Squadron badge. *66 Squadron* is seen climbing Parkstone Bank with the 9.15am Swanage–Waterloo service on 30 August 1958 when allocated to Bournemouth; it later moved to Exmouth Junction, where it was to remain until withdrawal. *K. L. Cook / Rail Archive Stephenson*

Right: A pleasing picture of *66 Squadron* as it heads an Exeter–Waterloo express along the four-track section near Brookwood during August 1960. *Derek Cross*

Left: A view inside Brighton Works shows Nos 34020 *Seaton* and 34101 *Hartland* receiving attention on 29 September 1956. The first of the rebuilt 'Merchant Navy' class, No 35018 *British India Line*, is also present, which was unusual for Brighton Works. No 35018 had been rebuilt the previous February.
*J. F. Davies /
Rail Archive Stephenson*

Below: No 34002 *Salisbury* is recorded receiving the finishing touches after its last general repair in March 1962 inside Eastleigh Works. Notice the amount of material dumped around on the floor near the engine, compared to the walkways in depots these days.
Pendragon Collection

In Works under Repair

Above: No 34005 *Barnstaple* was tested on the London Midland Region, working the 10.15am St Pancras– Manchester Central and 1.50pm return. It is shown near Redhill Tunnel, near Trent with the up working on 18 June 1948.
T. G. Hepburn /
Rail Archive Stephenson

Right: The locomotives selected for the trials were Nos 34004 *Yeovil*, 34005 *Barnstaple* and 34006 *Bude*, all of which visited Brighton Works before the trials. All were fitted with wedge-shaped cabs, speed recorders, longer smoke-deflectors and other items, with No 34004 getting a tablet-catcher for the Highland line. The class once again proved that there was nothing in the mixed traffic classes to beat them for steaming, but when it came to coal and water consumption they were bottom of the tables. *Yeovil* is seen here ready to leave Perth with the 4pm service for Inverness, its unlined black Stanier tender contrasting with its malachite-green livery.
Pendragon Collection

Above: No 34006 *Bude* worked test trains on the Western and Eastern regions. On the Western it was tested over the Devon banks on the 1.45pm Bristol–Plymouth working, returning the following day on the 1.35pm up service. On the Eastern it worked the 10am from Marylebone to Manchester, being shown leaving Marylebone on 8 June 1948. *F. R. Hebron / Rail Archive Stephenson*

Below: Another view of *Bude*, this time at Nottingham Victoria on 1 June 1948, as it heads the 8.20am service from Manchester London Road to Marylebone. An ex-Great Northern 'J6' 0-6-0 can be seen in the background. Nottingham Victoria closed on 4 September 1967. *J. P. Wilson / Rail Archive Stephenson*

Above: During its 13 years allocated to Nine Elms, No 34011 *Tavistock* waits to depart Waterloo with a Basingstoke train in February 1952. The route disc has yet to be placed in the correct position on the right-hand side of the smokebox. *Brian Morrison*

Right: A fine study taken on 23 January 1967 of No 34006 *Bude* inside Salisbury shed at night, clearly showing the large smoke-deflector plates. No 34006 was one of the three members of the class used in the 1948 Locomotive Exchanges. Records show it achieved the highest total mileage — 1,099,338 — of any member of the class. *D. Mackinnon*

Left: Deep inside Salisbury shed No 34056 *Croydon* appears to be well cleaned, but not in steam, on 23 January 1967. *D. Mackinnon*

Below: No 34002 *Salisbury* pictured at Salisbury station in the company of several young enthusiasts in October 1963. *G. F. Heiron/ Transport Treasury*

On Shed

Right: A fine study of No 34083 in malachite green with 'BRITISH RAILWAYS' on the tender, being turned on the turntable at Dover Marine ready to haul the 'Golden Arrow' Pullman. It was allocated to Stewarts Lane at the time and less than a year old. It was later named *605 Squadron. A. W. Croughton / Rail Archive Stephenson*

Below: Fresh from its last general overhaul, No 34019 *Bideford* is seen on shed at Eastleigh, ready to re-enter service, on 29 September 1961. It had four further visits to the works before its withdrawal in March 1967. A biplane can just be seen above the locomotive coming into land at the airport. *Gavin Morrison*

Above left: In immaculate external condition, the fireman looks down on the plaque on the cabside of *Royal Observer Corps* in July 1961 during the period when the locomotive was allocated to Bricklayers Arms shed. *Ian Allan Library*

Above: The fireman climbs aboard *145 Squadron* at Weymouth shed prior to working an up Channel Island boat train in 1966. *M. J. Esau*

Above: Four weeks before the end of steam at Salisbury shed *Bere Alston* and *Appledore* are seen side-by-side on 6 June 1967. *John Vaughan*

Above: Three weeks to go before the end of steam, but No 34057 *Biggin Hill* has already been withdrawn. Taken out of service six weeks earlier, it is seen on Nine Elms shed on 18 June 1967. *I. G. Holt*

Above right: Inside Ramsgate shed in 1949 is No 34068 *Kenley* alongside 'J'-class No 31595. *Kenley* went new to Ramsgate and stayed for two years before moving to Stewarts Lane. *D. Watkin / Rail Archive Stephenson*

Above: No 34103 *Calstock* went new to Stewarts Lane where it stayed for over six years. It is seen on shed being prepared for its next duty on 6 September 1953. *C. R. L. Coles / Rail Archive Stephenson*

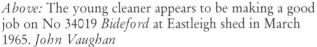

Above: The young cleaner appears to be making a good job on No 34019 *Bideford* at Eastleigh shed in March 1965. *John Vaughan*

Above: No 34100 *Appledore* receives attention inside Salisbury shed during the autumn of 1965. *John Vaughan*

Left: Six months before the end of its career, No 34066 *Spitfire* has been well coaled at Eastleigh shed when recorded on 19 March 1966. No 34066 was the locomotive involved in the disastrous accident at St Johns on 4 December 1957 when hauling the delayed 4.56pm Cannon Street–Dover service. Ninety people were killed and 108 badly injured in the accident, which was the result of delays caused by fog. *Gavin Morrison*

Right: Back in 1966 there was obviously an acute shortage of labour for cleaning up the shed yard at Bournemouth. *Blackmore Vale* is seen on 20 March of that year surrounded by ash, although the pit does appear to have been cleaned out. The locomotive was never actually allocated to Bournemouth but was a frequent visitor in the last few years of steam. It is in appalling external condition, but it did receive a light casual visit to Eastleigh Works three months later. It then lasted to the end of Southern steam before passing into preservation at the Bluebell Railway. *Gavin Morrison*

Below: Minus a shed plate, but allocated to Salisbury, No 34057 *Biggin Hill* stands on 18 April 1965 in the shed yard at Bournemouth. The main building of the shed can be seen in the background. No 34057 moved sheds 11 times during its career but never to Bournemouth. It lasted to within two months of the end of Southern steam and was subsequently sent to Cashmores for cutting up. *Gavin Morrison*

Above: Another view in Bournemouth shed yard, this time on 20 March 1966, shows No 34032 *Camelford* together with No 34021 *Dartmoor* ready to go off the shed. Neither locomotive was allocated to the shed; No 34032 was allocated at the time to Salisbury and No 34021 to Nine Elms. *Camelford* was withdrawn seven months later, whereas *Dartmoor* lasted to the end of steam. *Gavin Morrison*

Centre left: No 34009 *Lyme Regis* is shown at Eastleigh shed coaling plant seven months after rebuilding. It spent over half its career allocated to Nine Elms, which was its home depot at the time of this picture taken on 17 August 1961. *Gavin Morrison*

Left: No 34021 *Dartmoor* is pictured on 12 April 1963 outside its then home shed of Eastleigh awaiting its next turn of duty. It moved to Nine Elms in January 1965 where it remained until withdrawn in July 1967. *Gavin Morrison*

Above: It was very rare for a 'Royal Scot' and a 'West Country' to be seen together, but the view was captured on 30 April 1960 at Wembley Central on the occasion of the Schoolboys International football match. No 34010 *Sidmouth* is on a train for Brockenhurst, while 'Royal Scot' No 46112 *Sherwood Forester* is heading for Leicester. On the right is the rear end of a train to Lancashire.
C. R. L. Coles / Rail Archive Stephenson

Right: The 'Vectis Railtour' on 3 October 1965 visited the Lavant branch with two Bulleid 'Q1' class 0-6-0s, before heading for Portsmouth Harbour, where it is seen headed by an immaculate 'West Country' No 34002 *Salisbury*. A visit to the Isle of Wight followed, where Class O2 0-4-4Ts Nos 24 *Calbourne* and 14 *Fishbourne* took the special to Ventnor. Services beyond Shanklin to Ventnor ended on 18 April 1966.
Gavin Morrison

Right: Another view of No 34010 *Sidmouth*, this time in unrebuilt form, as it heads past Clapham Junction with an Ian Allan special to Exeter on 12 April 1953.
Brian Morrison

Left: A picture absolutely full of railway interest shows No 34066 *Spitfire* at Tunbridge Wells West station at the head of an RCTS/LCGB special on 22 March 1964. The locomotive shed can be seen in the background (right), whilst in the foreground is Class Q1 0-6-0 No 33027.
Hugh Ballantyne

Below: An unusual view of the LCGB 'Bridport Belle' shows the special entering Salisbury, headed by 'West Country' No 34102 *Lapford* and 'Battle of Britain' No 34057 *Biggin Hill* en route to Westbury from Waterloo on 22 January 1967.
Brian Stephenson

Right: A scene of great activity at Evercreech Junction on 2 January 1966 as a RCTS tour from Waterloo to Bath over the Somerset & Dorset pauses for water. Southern 'U'-class 2-6-0 No 31639 and 'West Country' No 34015 *Exmouth* took over the special at Broadstone from 'Merchant Navy' No 35011 *General Steam Navigation*. This was one of the many 'last' specials that ran over the S&D during its final year of operation. *Gavin Morrison*

Above: One of the famous RCTS 'East Midlander' specials, in this case No 4 of 11 September 1960, pauses for a locomotive change at Eastleigh station, whilst 'Battle of Britain' No 34090 *Sir Eustace Missenden, Southern Railway*, with the very large nameplate, waits to leave with a down train. As the BR 2-6-0 (No 76006) was taking the passengers to the works, the instruction on the Southern Railway board, prohibiting railwaymen from walking off the platform to the works yard and shed, would not have been broken. The train left Nottingham Victoria behind preserved Midland compound No 1000 to Oxford, where an ex-works Great Western Mogul (No 7317) took over for the run to Eastleigh. *Gavin Morrison*

Above: Apart from the Locomotive Exchanges in 1948, the furthest north that an unrebuilt member of the class ventured was when No 34094 *Mortehoe* reached Doncaster on a railtour. In the first of two pictures we see No 34079 *141 Squadron* well away from its usual haunts, just east of Stafford under the wires on the West Coast main line, on 16 June 1964.
M. Mensing

Left: Later the same day *141 Squadron* is seen on its journey back to Bristol, this time just south of Cannock, heading for Birmingham via Walsall.
M. Mensing

Right: The Southern Counties Touring Society 'Four Counties Special' speeds past Botley headed by No 34052 *Lord Dowding* (minus nameplates) on 9 October 1966.
John Vaughan

Right: A well groomed 'Battle of Britain', No 34088 *213 Squadron* allocated to Nine Elms, was chosen to work the first 'Regency Belle' Pullman train on 28 March 1964. The privately-operated train was marketed as the most exotic train in the world despite the use of a 'Brighton Belle' set. The train did not live up to expectations and was cancelled after four weeks due to a lack of patronage. *213 Squadron* is shown ready to leave Victoria for Brighton on 18 April 1964. The locomotive still possesses the fixing bolts on the smoke-deflector for 'Golden Arrow' duties. *G. D. King*

Above: Great Western enthusiasts in Devon and Cornwall were no doubt rather upset that a Southern Bulleid 'West Country' was chosen to haul the last steam working from Newton Abbot to Penzance and return on 3 May 1964. The trip was organised by the RCTS and Plymouth Railway Circle and here we see a well groomed No 34002 *Salisbury* at Plymouth North Road on the outward working. *Hugh Ballantyne*

Above: The semi-final of the FA Cup between Southampton and Manchester United at Villa Park in 1963 produced a number of specials, most of which were routed via Leamington, but this one travelled via Stourbridge Junction. This involved the train being double-headed for the climb through Old Hall station to the 896yd tunnel known as Blackheath or Old Hall. The unusual combination of ex-LMS '8F' No 48430 piloting rebuilt 'West Country' No 34046 *Braunton* makes a stirring sight as it passes Old Hall station with its 12 coaches on 17 April 1963. *M. Mensing*

Left: The third rail is clearly seen in this picture of No 34050 *Royal Observer Corps* as it heads the LCGB 'Wealdsman Rail Tour' past Dorking North on 13 June 1965. *Derek Cross*

Right: The LCGB 'Somerset-Dorset Rail Tour' — one of many in 1966 — probably had the most exciting motive power of all the specials. Two immaculately turned out unrebuilt Bulleid Light Pacifics — Nos 34006 *Bude* and 34057 *Biggin Hill* — did the honours. There was some superb late-evening lighting as shown in these two pictures which first shows the train climbing up the 1-in-50 gradient out of Bath to Devonshire Tunnel on 5 March 1966. Note the large smoke-deflectors fitted to No 34006. The train had been hauled from Waterloo to Templecombe by 'Merchant Navy' No 35028 *Clan Line*. At Templecombe two Ivatt 2-6-2Ts, Nos 41307 and 41249, took over for the trip to Glastonbury and back to Evercreech Junction.
Gavin Morrison

Above: The same day and about a mile further up the bank, the train is shown again glinting in the sunshine between Devonshire and Coombe Down tunnels. *Brian Stephenson*

Left: The 'Talyllyn Special', which was operated for the annual AGM of the preservation society, ran for many years and produced a variety of interesting motive power. On 28 September 1963 'Battle of Britain' No 34063 *229 Squadron* hauled the special north from Paddington. It is seen climbing the gradient at 1 in 164 out of High Wycombe to Saunderton. No 34063 had been allocated to Salisbury just 12 days earlier. *Brian Stephenson*

Above: The 'Royal Observer Corps' special train, appropriately headed by 'Battle of Britain' No 34050 in immaculate condition, approaches Woking Sidings with the empty stock from Farnborough on 13 September 1964. The locomotive was transferred to Eastleigh the following day so presumably had been prepared by its previous shed, Nine Elms. *Brian Stephenson*

Above: The end of Southern steam was only two months away on 7 May 1967 when the LCGB 'Dorset Coast Express' visited the Swanage branch, before carrying on to Weymouth. The train was topped-and-tailed along the branch by No 34023 *Blackmore Vale* and a dirty 2-6-4T No 80011. Photographed from the ramparts of Corfe Castle, the special heads back to Wareham past Norden, nowadays the northern terminus of the preserved Swanage Railway. *Gavin Morrison*

Right: With the Standard 2-6-4T having been detached, No 34023 *Blackmore Vale* is ready to leave Wareham for Weymouth. At Weymouth, the 'West Country' gave way to BR Standard Class 5MT No 73029 and Standard Class 4MT No 76026 for the return working up the hill to Dorchester. *Gavin Morrison*

Left: The 'Southern Rambler', complete with a wreath on the smokebox and shown as the last steam train from Eastbourne to Victoria, is seen near Plumpton with rebuilt 'West Country' No 34108 *Wincanton* on 19 March 1967. The locomotive had obviously received no special treatment for the occasion. *Brian Stephenson*

Above: Nos 34023 *Blackmore Vale* and 34108 *Wincanton* were both out again on 18 June 1967 on railtour duty. This time it was an RCTS special from Weymouth. The pair is seen climbing the gradient out of Weymouth to Dorchester past Upwey Wishing Well Halt. No 34108 had lost its nameplate in the last three months but was a little cleaner than in the previous picture; this could have been one of its last workings, as it was withdrawn during the month, whereas *Blackmore Vale* made it to the end of Southern steam and into preservation. *Brian Stephenson*